Ruthless Legacy

A Billionaire Boss Romance

Rebecca Baker

Copyright © 2024 by Rebecca Baker

All rights reserved.

No portion of this book may be reproduced in any form without written permission from the publisher or author, except as permitted by U.S. copyright law.

***

Sign up for my newsletter and receive a free romance novel:

https://sendfox.com/rebeccabaker

Contents

Chapter One	1
Chapter Two	7
Chapter Three	14
Chapter Four	20
Chapter Five	29
Chapter Six	35
Chapter Seven	42
Chapter Eight	50
Chapter Nine	57
Chapter Ten	64
Chapter Eleven	72
Chapter Twelve	80
Chapter Thirteen	88
Chapter Fourteen	97

Chapter Fifteen	107
Chapter Sixteen	115
Chapter Seventeen	122
Chapter Eighteen	128
Chapter Nineteen	134
Chapter Twenty	141
Chapter Twenty-One	148
Chapter Twenty-Two	157
Chapter Twenty-Three	165
Chapter Twenty-Four	171
Chapter Twenty-Five	177
Chapter Twenty-Six	184
Chapter Twenty-Seven	190
Chapter Twenty-Eight	196
Chapter Twenty-Nine	203
Chapter Thirty	211
Afterword	217
My free romance novel	218

Chapter One

RYDER

Elliot Perry is late.

I shift on the seat in his waiting room at his understated offices. The pretty receptionist has flirted, undone three buttons on her form-fitting top to let me admire her tits, and given me her number.

One I just might use.

I close my eyes. *No, Ryder, no.* That's the kind of shit that's gotten me sitting here in the first place.

Normally I wouldn't give a flying fuck about image. But apparently, others do. Including my father. Who's dead.

Happy fucking birthday to me.

"Mr. Sinclair?" The receptionist breathes the words in a way that would put Marilyn Monroe to shame, and as I stand, she flutters long eyelashes over green eyes that have to be tinted lenses.

Not that I care. The package is pretty, tempting, and put together by a masterful hand.

I saunter over to her and lean forward on the desk. "Your boss needs to learn time is money."

She leans in, giving me an interesting view right down into her cleavage, and the soft swell of those breasts are basically begging to be touched.

I'd like to touch them.

Pity taking her up on her offer is what they like to call a very bad idea, and I'm on a tight schedule. But I take the time to smile and wink at Lena—according to the nameplate—not just because she's curvy and hot and willing, but I know the supposedly inconsequential people are always way more important than one might suspect. I know of deals that have fallen by the wayside because a mail guy didn't like how the prospective client spoke to them.

Not me.

Besides, I'd totally do her.

Four weeks. That's all. Four weeks of good behavior.

And then I'll finally have my slice of the family heritage pie.

"Which way, Lena?"

Her hand flutters as she points down the small, plain hall on the fifth floor of the offices nestled in the heart of SoHo. "To your left."

"Gotcha."

I stride down and see the nameplate in discreet gold letters. Elliot Perry.

This dude is meant to be the best, so good most people haven't heard of him. And he's what I think I'm going to need.

I give a perfunctory knock, then open the door, stepping into the art deco styled room. Cozy and understated. The kind of look that says competence, confidence, and discretion.

The parquet floor glows and shows off its intricate design of dark and pale woods, the desk is a high gloss satinwood with rounded edges and small detailing. It looks original, a Ruhlmann if I'm not mistaken. And the chairs with their wide matching curves and burnt orange leather backs and seats are gorgeous.

The paneled glass window that looks out over Prince Street and its wintry-like day draws the eye, as does the mirror edged in black and gold with a graceful silhouetted Twenties woman on it that's more art than function. It sits to the right on another curved table, this one higher, with a growing orchid, slender, beautiful in its purple shades balancing it out.

There's a lady palm to the left and a long, curved deco sofa against the far wall.

And no one inside.

I glance about and see a door. It's tucked to the far right along the way, and when it's shut, you might not see it. But it's open and bright light spills out.

I sit in the chair opposite the desk and cross my legs, pulling my phone from my pocket to check the day's schedule I already have in my head. I don't mind waiting, but not for this kind of shit. So I clear my throat.

"My time's tight today," I say, "so if you don't mind, I'll start."

No answer, but I hear, above the sound of traffic swishing through the wet street from the rain earlier, water running.

"Four weeks. I need you to turn me into a boring, solid pillar of fucking society."

Boring. That's the word.

"I've heard you're the best. And that's what I need. It has to seem natural, like I'm on a path of self-discovery or growth or whatever floats their boat." I check the time on my phone. "I just need to look good, and then we can go pick up chicks to celebrate when those four weeks are done."

Seriously, I don't know why I say this. I've never met this guy. I don't know if I want to hang with him after four weeks of keeping me on the straight and narrow and away from pussy, of making me shine. I don't even know if he's married or got a piece or what.

I'm just irritated he's not here, facing me, so I'm pushing buttons.

I'm also irritated I can't tap the receptionist, who's about a mile above most I meet. And I'm even more annoyed that I can't fuck the blonde babe I met right after I got the rude and unnecessary hauling over the coals. Not the first one, the last one, that came with the letter from dear old dead Dad.

Last night.

I'm hung over, grumpy, and don't want to be here, so acting like some small child.

But I also want this, so pissed off or not, here I am. Trying to figure out if this Elliot Perry is worth my time or if I should see what else is out there.

What am I thinking? This isn't exactly a service provided on LinkedIn. At least not one that provides what I want.

And time is of the essence. I'm here. I need this guy to be what I need.

"Picking up chicks, as you so charmingly put it, really isn't my jam, Sinclair."

The voice, rich with a hint of smoke and spice rolls through me.

Two things are immediately apparent by the voice.

One—Elliot Perry's got attitude.

Two—Elliot Perry is most certainly not male.

Three—I didn't do my homework.

Yeah. Make that three.

"That's either Mr. Sinclair," I say, keeping my tone casual, confident and laid back, the one that has panties dropping in a half-mile radius. "Or Ryder. I'd suggest some kind of pet name, but I don't think we're going to have that kind of relationship."

Heels click on the floor as the merest hint of gardenias floats about me. "I'm not sure we'll be having any relationship at all."

"Why?" I don't turn. I don't do the sort of thing like handing people like her all the power. That's what turning around will do, and since she's going to be guiding me in my life, exactly where I don't want outsiders, even ones I hire, I'm not giving everything up. "Not enough money?"

"I'm not sure I have enough to work with."

I smile. She sounds tall and willowy, with the kind of breasts a man can lose himself in. And long legs. I'm picturing a smoldering beauty, dressed to match this place, dressed like elegant sex, a hot woman who can get real dirty when she's played just right. I'm seeing long black hair, loose, and—

"Interesting. Why are you smiling?"

My imagination is a little too free and easy.

"Because you sound like you're testing me."

"I'm doing nothing of the sort. I'm highly discreet, I'm top of my game, and I take on clients of my choosing. You're lucky I let you in."

She leans against the desk and crosses her arms over her tits. My imagination got those spot on. Lush and full. Like her body. Some might say plump, but I don't mind that. I like them all shapes, all sizes, as long as the woman is beautiful and willing and knows my game.

But the rest of her?

She's plain. A wide mouth, pointed little nose, and red hair that's pinned back in some kind of hell bun. She wears dark gray wide trousers with those heels, and a tie and buttoned up shirt.

There's intelligence in her face that makes her interesting, and her soft gold eyes are full of fire. She's more interesting than beautiful. Or could be.

And again, I'm not here to score. I'm here to win.

"I could buy your company a hundred times over."

She laughs. "Why on Earth would you do that? You're in real estate."

"I like to invest."

"Does your kind understand the value of quality?"

I narrow my eyes because this is going dark, wild places. "Are you calling me shallow?"

"Does the nine hundred dollar loafer fit?"

"How dare you." I should be pissed off, but I'm not. She's fun. "I've never worn a loafer in my life. And what about you? With your try-hard art deco pieces?"

Her mouth twitches as she drops her arms to rest on the edge of the desk next to her hips. "I like art deco. I like style."

"So do I." I clear my throat and look up at her from my seat. "I think we got off on the wrong foot. I'm in need of your services. Four weeks."

"You want the pig's ear to silken purse treatment?"

"If that means staid and boring and someone who's responsible and able to carry their family's flagship, then yes."

This time, she laughs. Then the laughter fades. "Tell me why I should take you on."

A lot of reasons go through my head, but I dismiss them all. I go for the truth.

"My esteemed late father decided to set out a task for each of his sons. And when we get our letter, we have four weeks to prove we have what it takes."

"Save me from the mega rich."

I ignore her tone and words on account I need her magic touch.

"The infamous and rumored Sinclair jewels are real and we're each getting a piece. A family heirloom, basically. For some reason I can't fathom, this is tied up with the Sinclair real estate flagship. The original company. It seems my job is to prove I can be responsible and upstanding. Enough to please the stipulations laid out by the board."

She looks at me like she doesn't like me much. Which is insane. She doesn't know me. And, she's a woman. "So you miss out on an expensive piece of jewelry if you don't do this."

"It's an heirloom. Beyond monetary value. Part of my family history. And the company hangs in the balance. It's private now; the shares fall on my family's side. If I fail, if I don't prove I'm capable of being figurehead—" I'm pretty damn sure that didn't come from anyone other than Jenson and my mother "—then the balance of shares will go public and it won't be our company."

Elliot looks anything but impressed. "You're loaded. Buy it."

"I can't. There are stipulations and rules."

Those were my fathers, I think. But this whole figurehead crap, I know my mother's somehow behind this. How much and why…I'll find out.

"And," I add, "I don't want to let my family down."

"Your scandal didn't help."

"I don't need you to point that out. Just help me do this."

She taps her fingers against the desk. "Isn't getting help outside the rules?"

"No. I just have to do it. Any way, any means." Fuck, I'm going to have to say it. "I can't do it on my own."

And then she does something I don't think a woman's ever done.

She turns me down.

Cold.

Chapter Two

ELLIOT

The look on his face when I say no is a photo worthy moment.

"What do you mean?"

"It's a simple, yet important word. No. I've got better things to do than hold the hand of a billionaire."

"You helped Chris Leone! You got him elected." He gives me a thoughtful look, at odds with his outraged tone.

Yes, I did. Long ago, and that bastard, one of the people I built my reputation on by being invisible, powerful, and able to deliver the undeliverable, haunts me.

"Look—"

"It's four weeks. Four weeks. For a family company. A necklace. They mean something to me. I'm not changing the world. I'm not trying to bring it down."

My mouth is dry.

I can't work for Ryder Sinclair.

What sane, living, breathing heterosexual woman with no chance in hell—not that I want a chance—would?

His photos don't do him justice. In those, he's gorgeous, charismatic; I know, because the media loves him. Rich and hot and a bad boy.

But what they don't capture is the fact he's devastating. The height; I'm tall enough at five eleven, and he's about six three; the lean, hard lines of him; the elegance: those are more pronounced.

Beyond that, he's arresting. Thick, softly curling charcoal hair that borders on too long, but perfect for sliding fingers into while kissing or during sex. Dark chocolate melting eyes that hold a wicked light, a sensuous mouth that looks made to kiss and do other things to a woman that should be illegal but thank goodness aren't. And he's hard, dangerous, and decadent. They shouldn't exist together, but they do, and the combination is irresistible.

There's absolutely no way I can work with him.

Normally, men like him don't even get more than a blip on my radar, but he makes it go haywire. He's too good looking, too aware of that, and he exudes sex. Not smarm, but that animalistic undercurrent that's just him. And he looks at you.

Like he sees you.

Like you're important.

I know it's one of his moves. A man like that never notices a woman like me. That's not insecurity, that's experience.

I'm tall and red-headed and people don't notice me. That's fine, it suits my business down to the ground. I know it's some kind of feat to be tall with this hair and still go about unnoticed. Call it a miracle of the world.

And he...

Yeah, he's the quintessential bad boy rich guy. Spoiled, and thinks he can do whatever he wants. Actually, I take that back. He can do anything he wants; he's so loaded it's almost unbelievable and I'm not hurting at all.

"I don't really care," I say. I get up and walk around the desk, aware his gaze eats into my every move. Jesus, does every woman who crosses his path feel like this? I'm betting it's a yes, and that includes grandmothers and the happily relationshipped. I take a seat and settle back, keeping my game face switched on with added defenses.

"I'm not asking you to care."

"You're asking me to do a job I don't want to do."

A small smile plays over that sensual mouth. "Why?"

"It doesn't interest me."

The smile grows. "If that's your attitude, Perry, then I'm wondering how you made it this far."

"Asking if I fucked my way to the top?"

The asshat laughs. "You? No."

I stand and so does he. But anger and the meaning of his words fuel my move. I'm not sure why he does it, though I doubt it's out of politeness. "I think we're done."

"You might be, but I'm not," he says, "and I meant you don't look the type." Ryder shrugs. "Not that there's anything wrong with it. If sleeping your way anywhere floats your boat."

"Is that what you did?"

He laughs again. "Perhaps fucked my way down to here."

"I'm still not interested."

His laughter dies and Ryder gives me a considering look. "It's an easy job."

It should be, but I know it won't be. He's charming even when he's an asshole, like he was at the start, and I really don't need the grief. He likes women too much. As in, get down and dirty with a new one every day, and... Shit.

He's too damn good looking and I'll develop an unwanted crush on him and it's going to be awful. If I take the job. Which I won't.

"Ryder, I see the papers. I read the stuff online. And you're the party boy, the guy who takes nothing and no one seriously. There's a line of women gagging for it—" his brows rise when I say this "—and you don't care if they're married, in a relationship, or anything. If it's female, and you want her, you go for it. Getting you to keep it in your pants is going to be a losing battle. With extra headache thrown in."

He doesn't say a word, simply crosses his arms. "You've got me all figured out, I see."

"Am I wrong?"

"It shouldn't matter."

He's right, it shouldn't. Not in the grand scheme of things. But I promised myself a few things when I started having enough money to walk away from jobs if I chose.

I promised not to take on the monsters.

I promised not to take on unnecessary headaches or clients who were pushed into my hands.

I promised not to torture myself.

He'll be torture.

I know myself well enough to know a man that hot, that charming, that bad-boy-to-the-bone will appeal on a molecular level.

Shallow, yes. But hormones and pretty and sex appeal don't care about depth.

I won't like him and I'll tangle up in stupid hormonal responses to him.

And he won't even notice me.

Not that I want that.

"It shouldn't, but..." I can't say that to him. I'm not an idiot. "Chances are this is going to be an above and beyond job. Chances are you'll fail."

"So I fail and you look bad? No one except those in the know know you." He rubs a hand over his eyes and shakes his head. "That sounds like a bad song."

"I'm choosy with clients I take on. I have someone who works for me. Andre. He's excellent and he—"

"No. I want you."

I sigh. And my pulse starts to beat hard. He wants my expertise. Nothing more, nothing less. "But you can't have me."

His dark chocolate eyes meet mine and everything goes into freefall. The look is pure sex and he knows it. Imagine if he really turned that dial to on.

"This is important," he says. "I want the best. So I want you. Jillian Cohen gave me your name."

Beautiful, smart, talented, and a female version of him. I don't swing that way, so working with her had been difficult but doable. No lust.

"And yes, we did, in case you're wondering," he says this like he's discussing the weather. "I don't have photos. Well, none I'm willing to share."

"Your name never came up."

"I met her after you turned her into the respected anchorwoman she is now."

I pick up the sleek black and gold antique pen on my desk. "And she gave you my details?"

That's how it worked, word of mouth. I moved years ago from PR into this strange little niche and found people wanted to pay me a fortune to sprinkle fairy dust on their lives and make them into something else.

"You're moralistic?"

"No. Not like that. And Jillian should never have needed to hire me. She's smart and—"

"You know how the world works. No one can do a thing, or have done or said anything without it biting them in the ass. Hey, I never did any soft porn."

"Neither did Jillian." He just looks at me.

I get his point. I made a lot of that go away. And without lies. I trained her how to own her past, downplay it, and reinvent herself.

"You don't even need someone like me. Do you care what others think? She did. To a point. And that matters."

He crosses to the window and stares out. "Think of me what you want, Elliot. You will anyway, and I don't care about most opinions. I do my job, I do it well. I can be responsible in business and have a good time."

"You like having a really good time."

"Not a crime."

He's right. It isn't. But I'm not turning him down for that. I've also turned people down for so many different reasons or handed them to Andre because I could, because I wanted to, because I didn't like them. But I don't think I've ever turned someone down over a very probable crush.

And not one of those people have fought me on it when I said no.

"Lena can help you find someone else if Andre doesn't meet your expectations. There are excellent PR companies and contractors who are discreet and also specialize in this sort of thing."

"Those," he says, not looking at me, and even his profile is gorgeous, "are lies. No one does what you do the way you do it. If I wanted just PR who specialized in this sort of thing, I'd have it. This needs your touch. And yeah, I need you to help me not step out of line. No dates unless they're the right ones, no fucking around—"

"No scandal."

"—for four weeks." He runs a finger along the glass like he's tracing the line of the building opposite. "And I don't seek out scandal."

"That wasn't your first."

"That was complicated."

"True love got interrupted, did it?"

He shoots a dirty glance my way. "Hardly love. And it's in the past. Ever since I was a kid, I've been fascinated by the Sinclair jewels. Now they turn up. And my family heritage is important. These things are worth more than money. They belong to the family. They're part of my past and I want them to be part of my future. And apparently, I have to prove I'm worthy. That I can be the figurehead of the company, which means not being me. Four weeks. That's all."

"And then you go back to your old ways?"

"Well, I'm not planning on becoming a monk." The corner of his mouth tilts up into a smile. "But I'm not about to give a big fuck you to the board and my mother by having an orgy in Times Square."

I laugh in spite of myself. "That's quite the image."

"My point is, I'm not planning to screw up the work we do by fucking about, or anything like that. I want this. But I need your help."

"To stop you fucking about."

Ryder doesn't answer immediately, then finally, he turns, those melting chocolate eyes on me and I can barely breathe. "What answer do you want?"

"You're just interested in chasing skirt, more than any of this."

"Old fashioned of you." He glances about and dips his head a little, but I see the slow grin. "To clarify, I'm way more interested in what lies beneath the skirt I'm chasing. But no sweet pussy is about to get in my way of what I want. The letter stipulates me being on the straight and narrow and the boring high road straight into morality town. Should be right up your shiny and pristine alley."

"You have no idea what my alley is like." I glare. He's annoying right there along with the charm and hotness as sex appeal.

Hate crush. Fantastic. I can feel the simmering heat of electric push pull to him already.

"So the letter says be a monk for a month."

He pulls a thick piece of folded paper from the inner pocket of his divine and no doubt bespoke three piece suit. It's completely unsuitable for the kind of thing he's talking about, a wild silk purple paisley on the inside and the material itself for the outer suit is a dark, soft red with a subtle black and purple plaid. It's, in short, outrageous for business. And it's completely devastating on him.

Ryder hands it to me. The paper, not the suit. That, he keeps on.

I scan the letter, and it's everything he said. I just hand it back and he puts it away.

"As you see, it doesn't say that, but scandal free and not making a lot of women happy is something I've been told I have to do. Which is why I'm here. So, take the damn job."

"No."

That's self-preservation speaking, right there.

He looks me up and down. "I'll pay you five times your asking price."

I stare at him. If I were a weaker woman, I'd fall to the ground.

That's...that's an astronomical amount of money.

The fee I set Ryder Sinclair was already outrageous because he's Ryder Sinclair and I figured if the billionaire wanted my services he'd have to pay.

Then I met him and realized I couldn't do it.

But for that kind of money?

I can't say no.

"Okay." I get up and cross to him. "I'll do it. But there are going to be ground rules. Follow them, or I walk."

Chapter Three

RYDER

The woman is a barracuda.

I don't care about parting with that much money, and she's looking at me like I've lost my mind. I probably have. I'm more than aware that what I'm paying her would buy some rare and fine jewels, but this isn't about money.

This is about history. My heritage. Something important to me.

Most think I only care about women, sex, fun, and money. And they're not wrong, as I do care about those things. I like having a good time. Sue me. But I care about the intangible, too. Our family's name and company belong to the family. And these Sinclair jewels? They're important more than for whatever they're worth. They're our history.

"So what do we do?"

Her smile is cool and she looks at me like I'm not Ryder Sinclair. She looks at me like she might look at her UPS guy. Actually, I'm betting she gives him a far warmer welcome. For some reason she doesn't like me, but I really don't care either way.

She gestures to the door. "I'll courier a contract to you tonight. Sign, make the first payment—"

"You don't think I can pay?"

"I think you might need to learn others follow protocol."

I nod. "I can do that. Time is short, though."

"After you courier it back to me, we'll get started." Elliot Perry once again gestures at the door. "Lena will get all your details I need."

And then, like I no longer exist, she sits back at her desk and starts working on her laptop.

The next four weeks are going to be interesting.

The Lower East Side upscale bar we're at is one of those faux grunge places that border the East Village and all the rich, cool young things are here. Along with my brothers.

Magnus is with the little sweet thing he's chosen to marry in the next few months. My black hearted, career-oriented brother found an actual heart, and a reason for having one. Zoey is also as steely as him and stubborn beneath the sweetness, and my brother still occasionally gets a look like he doesn't quite believe what happened to him.

Then there's Hudson and Scarlett, who are married, in love, and judging from the hovering he's doing and her alcohol-free zone, I'm betting there's a future Sinclair baking away in her oven.

There's only me and Kingston who remained blissfully untethered.

King's as cynical as they come, and his interest in the jewels is purely monetary. He's already got plans of a display if he can only talk the other two into lending the pieces that adorn both Zoey and Scarlett.

"You're really gonna do it, Ry?" he asks, taking a swallow of his whiskey.

I raise my own in a silent salute. "Yeah, it's four weeks and I'm intrigued what mother dearest's role is in this."

"She needs a hobby," says Magnus, whose comment earns an elbow in the ribs from Zoey, who sits on the arm of his sofa-like chair. "Well, she does, Zo."

"I'm betting a thousand he can't."

Scarlett looks at Hud. "Well, I don't know. Ryder might be made of stronger stuff. Team Ryder."

I'm about to thank her when a hot woman walks in. She's got short black hair and a roll to her hips that does things to a man. Her smile sets off mine and Hudson says, "Actually, make it five hundred thousand."

Kingston smooths out the letter on his jean-clad thigh and he looks at it and then at me. "You gotta stop that shit if you want this. Maybe the company is sitting on something huge we don't know about."

"Like what? We're board members. No, this shit is nothing more than games with things we care about—I care about."

"Not against what's happened to me, and I think I speak for Hud, too," says Magnus, "but our father always liked to play stupid games."

"Maman," I say, with a heavy emphasis on the sarcastic as she prefers mother for reasons of her own, "also does. You can't tell me she's hands free."

"Not with you, that's for sure." Hud laughs. "You got it good over that scandal."

"I warned you to quit that shit," says Mag.

"Yeah, well, I'm thirty-two. What the hell does what I do have to do with how I perform in my work roles?"

"Father from beyond."

"Thanks, King."

He shrugs. "We've been waiting for the next one. It's you, and if you want the necklace and to keep the company, then..."

Yeah. Play by the manipulative rules. No one needs to tell me that. Just put a collar on me and call it a day. Still, Elliot Perry's going to definitely be interesting.

"I hired someone to help me."

King raises a brow. I'm not going to tell him how much money I'm spending, he'll think I'm an idiot.

"You think you need help?"

The music in this place goes up a notch. Nothing special, just indie vibes on the right side of upbeat. I lean in a little closer so I'm not shouting. "Yes."

Kingston starts laughing and hands me back the letter. "Oh, man, you can do without sex for four weeks. Actually, who said you needed to do that?"

"Clean up my act came straight from the matriarch's mouth." And a note that came with the letter, a note I haven't shown anyone. Jenson's hand, directed no doubt by my mother as I highly doubt they held a séance. A note that says no screwing about. "That's what the rest of the board wants, and we're not included in that balance."

Another fucking rule from the great beyond, during this, the balance of the shares reside with the rest of the shareholders. But I'm refusing to go there.

Four weeks. It can't be that hard, not with Elliot breathing fire on me.

"Maybe this is a new start for you," Zoey says, shouting over the music.

I'm not about to say how I feel in front of her, that a new start where I have to go without or tie myself down is a fate worse than death, because I know what she means.

"I just want my piece of the Sinclair jewels. They must be worth an insane amount," says Kingston. "So don't fuck this up."

We have more drinks and Hudson and Scarlett leave, then Zoey and Magnus who get that look. It's just me and King and that hot dark-haired woman that's at the periphery, surrounded by men. And she's sending me all the right signals.

"Who did you hire?"

"Someone called Elliot Perry."

He frowns. "I don't know him."

"It's four weeks and then we'll have this in the bag, and then it's your turn."

"Yeah." Kingston turns his glass in his hands. "My turn. I'm not interested in games. I have other things to do with my time. So let's get to the bottom of this and then I get my jewels. We'll value them and if it works in our favor, we'll let one of the museums display them. People have talked about them for years."

"They're beautiful."

He shoots me a look. "So? That means zero. The most expensive jewels are pretty gaudy in modern lighting. Or just gaudy. I want to know how much they all are worth."

"Hudson and Magnus might not let them go for you."

"I'm very persuasive."

He is. "You think I can do it?"

"Do I think you can keep your dick dry? No. But you can practice discretion."

"My moves are going to be watched."

"That they are." He checks his watch. "I have to get out of here. Hot date."

"Are you seeing someone?"

"Not really sure yet. I'll see how it plays out. She's fun right now. Stay at this level and all is good. Catch you later."

When he goes, long, slender legs in a short skirt slide past me and the dark-haired woman with the hips and searing looks takes his seat. Her top is tight and shows off her perfect handfuls of tits.

"You're hot, so am I," she says in a practiced purr. "How about you get us a drink?"

This is so ingrained in me I signal the cocktail waitress and order whatever she's having and another whiskey for me before I realize what I'm doing.

Still, a little light flirting won't hurt, right? No one expects me to be a monk. I don't think anyone would believe it. But this is a chick I'll spend some hours getting sweaty and sharing orgasms with and never bothering to know more than her name and some light conversation.

Already my resolve slips. Am I meant to be starting now? Or in the morning?

Jesus, Ryder, I think. *You're a fuck up.*

One who knows how to have a good time.

I couriered back the contract but I haven't heard from Elliot and it's heading towards eleven pm. So...

Flirting is fine. I'm in public.

The woman slides her fingers down my arm. I think she mentioned her name, but I can't remember it. She's everything Elliot Perry isn't. Beautiful, overtly sexy and knows it, and down for fun.

"So what do you do, Ryder?"

I didn't tell her my name, but I let it slide. If she wants to pretend she doesn't know who I am, more power to her. I'm not about to put a ring on her finger. I'm not about to enter into anything like a relationship with her.

Hell, I'm probably not going to be anywhere private with her, either.

"This and that," I say. "You?"

She leans in and starts talking. I'm going to have to have words with Jillian. We fucked about a number of times a few years back and stayed friendly. I'm friendly with most of the women I bone. Some hope for another chance, others just know the score and we like each other.

But Jillian's the one who I see the most in some of the circles I move in. And when she told me about Elliot Perry when I called her, she forgot to mention the red hair and the most interesting mouth I've seen.

Wide, soft, with a sharp, intelligent tongue.

Yeah, Elliot has the most intriguing mouth I've ever met.

If one can meet a mouth.

The woman's stopped talking and her hand is on my thigh, warm and high enough that she's not interested in subtle.

I meet her brown eyes. "What do you say we take our combined hotness out of here and to somewhere a lot more private?"

Shit. I want to. I shouldn't. It's a physical thing. She's going to bore me after sex, I'm aware of that.

"Well, thing is, I—"

My phone lights up. It's a number I don't recognize, but I know who it is.

Time to begin, Sinclair.

Something in me relaxes as something else tightens and I pick up the woman's hand and place it on the arm of the chair.

"I'd love to," I say, trying to keep the relief from my voice, "but business calls."

And with that, I get up, pay my bill and get the fuck out.

When and where?

To my utter shock, I'm looking forward to working with Elliot Perry.

Chapter Four

ELLIOT

I'm not sure what possessed me to contact Ryder Sinclair this evening. But here I am, in the East Village on Second Avenue and East Fifth.

It's a wine bar, Italian, and not too over the top.

I take a breath. I'm looking forward to this as much as I look forward to a root canal. Still, I push open the door and it takes me about zero seconds to spot Ryder.

"Do you need a table?"

"I have a table." I flash a smile I don't feel at the hostess and make my way to the tall, slim table with the slender metal stools.

Ryder sits on one and a blonde is draped over the other. And my heart sinks because I know this is what he's like, what he'll be like, and I was swayed by money.

Make that root canal without the lidocaine.

He looks up and the blonde does too, but she dismisses me with a shake of her hair and her hand on his. Her red dress is the type I'd never wear, short and tight and imagination-free.

But Ryder leans in to her and says something and the woman gets up and prances off. He gestures to the seat and I take the other one.

"Are you some kind of dark horse or do you have a killer work ethic?" he asks. There's a soft smile at play on his killer mouth and a glint in his eyes that says he knows exactly why I didn't sit where his blonde babe sat.

"Because I wanted to see you now?"

"Something like that."

The waiter comes by and I order a house white I've no intentions of drinking.

"No," I say, when we're alone, "I just believe in ripping the band aid off."

"Ouch." He smiles and gives me a low-lidded look that's pure smolder and it hooks me down deep in my sex. "Maybe you'll find maybe I'm not that bad."

"You're worse." I give him my coolest glare that's so arctic it's a wonder he hasn't frozen solid. "And stop flirting."

"Darling Elliot, you'll know when I decide to flirt with you."

I can't work with this man. But I have to. And this is why I called the meeting. I don't usually do it so late, or before we've set up rules, but he's different, and he has trouble all over him.

Me seeing my clients in their relaxed, natural state is something I have to do and I guess I've answered my own question on what possessed me. Ryder Sinclair is different from the others. He'll hide if I go and set up the rules first.

Most people don't hide. They don't want to change. Or don't want to pretend to change, even if they say they do. He's no different in that. But Ryder's a master at manipulation and hiding to get what he wants, when he wants. He's the hottest man I've met, yes, but he's got to be all that if he remains on good terms with the women he sleeps with. I spent a good few hours making calls and reaching out under the pretext of writing an article.

And every woman I spoke to sighed. Every woman had a smile in her voice. And every woman, even Lacey Fox, the one from his most recent scandal, all had nothing but good things to say about him.

Even Lacey. Whose marriage is blowing up all over media. Of course, that probably suits her and her husband, but still, she didn't dish dirt to further her career. At least, not on Ryder.

"No flirting. That's off the table."

He gives me a pained look and sips his wine. "It's in my DNA."

"Get it out of your DNA."

"I'm not sure I can do that, and how is flirting against the rules?"

My drink arrives and I resist the urge to play with my glass. "Flirting is when flirting always leads to more."

"That isn't true."

"Isn't it?" I give him a considering look. "You're telling me you'd have turned her down if I hadn't turned up?"

"I wouldn't have been here."

"That isn't an answer."

"It's the one you have."

He's not going to help himself, even if he wanted to. This man, he does this shit without thought because it is part of him, and he can hide it, I think, but perhaps not in the way that he needs to help him.

"You want to change," I say. "Or change long enough and well enough to make it convincing, so your style of flirting with intent has to stop. We need to set up..."

I trail off. He's nodding at my words, making murmurs of agreement, but he's not paying attention. His body language gives him away. Ryder's focused on the room beyond me, on the women who are giving him the eye.

I don't need to turn to see that. There's a flicker of response in his face, subtle and not for me, a welcoming, fuck me kind of fleeting expression that probably gives underwear companies all kinds of thrills if they knew what he did to their merchandise.

His gaze shifts back to me as the pause goes on long enough. "Set up what?"

"A game plan. That includes your behavior, attitude, standing, body language, and any alien lifeforms you deem appropriate. Sound good?"

"Sure."

I nod. Then I push back my stool, rise and walk out into the busy nightlight of the East Village.

"Elliot."

I slow my pace and then stop.

"Elliot?"

Slowly I turn and look at him. He has his jacket in one hand, and the sleeves to his sweater are slightly pushed up, ink showing from above the wrist on the left one. Of course Ryder Sinclair has tattoos.

"You pay me an astronomical fee to turn your life into something you need it to be. If you sabotage that, I still get paid."

"I'm not—"

"You were in there," I say, stalking up to him, "flirting and not paying attention to me. The first tells me you don't take anything but a good time seriously. The second, that you don't take me seriously. And that means we have a problem."

Ryder shrugs. "I like fun. That's why it's called fun and not work. And I do take you seriously."

"No, you don't. And if you don't focus, I'll walk. You need me way more than I need you and your money." I say this quietly. "Actually, I don't need your money."

"Okay, fine. And I know what I was doing. I wanted to see what you're like, what you see. This is my life I'm putting in your hands."

"Do you do that to everyone?"

He rubs the back of his neck. "Put my life in other people's hands?"

"Test them like you were doing to me."

"You were testing me."

"It's my job to assess and work out the best approach. I don't take your word for it. Otherwise I'd be doing baseline PR work."

"No," he says, finally, "I don't put my life in anyone's hands. And yes, I like to see who and what I'm working with. In all aspects."

I should end it now, cut my losses. Walk.

And Ryder smiles his melting smile that floors me.

"C'mon, Elliot. We'll start again. I know a place."

Against my better judgment, I say okay. We end up walking through the streets from the East Village to SoHo. We're on Wooster Street between Houston and Prince, close to my office, but he pushes open a door to a bar I don't even know is there and we go in. It's quiet, no nonsense and old school. Not new SoHo vibe.

I give him a considering look as we descend the short staircase into the dark wood lined bar. No loud music, just something low that fits with the mood of drinks and conversation.

"No flash? No glamor? No hot babes for you to take your pick from?"

"My life isn't just all that," he says as we go to the bar and take a seat. "Sometimes it's good to know places where no one gives a shit about you."

He orders an Old Fashioned and I do the same for convenience.

"Tomorrow we need to get you a different wardrobe. And with meetings, don't simply be on time, be early, prepared, and ready to work."

Ryder leans in, those dark eyes warm on me. "Are we really talking work?"

"This isn't a date."

"I don't date."

No, I'm betting he doesn't. He hooks up. "You hired me, and we need to get the basics down."

"Boring suits, we can do that if I must. But they need to be beautiful." Again those eyes touch on me, this time my mouth and I've never wanted to lean in and steal a kiss before in my life like I do now. Because I'm betting he tastes even better than he looks. "And I know how to work. I know how to make an impression. The right impression. More so, I know how to do a job."

"Your reputation doesn't reflect that."

"So?"

"So, it needs to."

He sighs. "There are more interesting things we could be doing than talking about this."

His words hit hard, and my breath stalls in my throat.

"Don't flirt."

"I'm just being me, Perry, that's all."

Or he's pushing my buttons. I don't believe for a second he's being him. I'm not the type—if he has a type—he flirts with.

What am I thinking? Of course he has a type. Beautiful. Confident. Natural attention beacons. Like Jillian, like Lacey, like the woman in the red dress, like every single one I managed to track down and speak to. He might not go for a certain build or coloring or height, but he goes for absolute stunners. Every time.

The drinks arrive and Ryder places a hundred on the bar. I glance at him.

"I'm not showing off. It's what I have and this place doesn't do plastic or digital. It's old school."

I pick up the drink and take a sip for something to do. It's perfect. I'll give the man this, he likes quality.

"Tonight's about the rules. I'll go over them again tomorrow—"

"No sleeping about, no flirting and not even with you, work hard, be early and you'll be fitting me with a gilded cage right after the shopping spree."

"I was thinking plain iron bars."

"You have no soul. Gilded."

"Tacky."

He clinks his glass to mine. "We'll agree to disagree."

"I'm not getting pulled down into your charm."

"You think I'm charming."

"It's a version of charm." I stop myself. I'm verging on flirting with him, and that's dangerous. Not to mention completely a waste of time. "Basically, while we spend some time together in the next couple of days, those are the ground rules. I'm going to get to know you a little better. And you're not going to make a decision outside of work without my approval."

"Are you offering to be my babysitter, Elliot?"

"I need control—"

"No. I see my brothers. I go out. I—"

"Get yourself embroiled in scandal. We'll work on that all tomorrow. Right now, I need to know about you. Family, schooling, skeletons in your closet."

He nods slowly and then leans an elbow on the bar. "All my skeletons are strictly closet-free."

"No friends?"

"I have friends, but I don't hang out on a regular basis like I do with my brothers."

"I find that hard to believe."

"What about you?"

"We're not here to talk about me," I say with a frown, fingers going tight on my cold glass.

His gaze is back on my mouth again. "Maybe we should."

"Maybe we should stick to the plan."

"I'm the youngest of four. My parents split when I was maybe six." He downs his drink and I get the feeling he knows exactly when and this is his spiel.

"My mother never remarried. My father had a string of ex-wives, younger and younger and all unnervingly similar to our mother. And for some reason they remained close. My parents. Not my father and his exes. We were instilled with a work ethic from him early on."

"And you rebelled?"

"Some might say I've got his eye for the ladies." He pauses. "Although they don't look like my mother. That would be weird."

I laugh, I can't help it. "Positively Oedipal."

"And look what happened there." He pauses again. "You know I went to Princeton, but I got in on my own merit. I worked for it. That was the rule. We work for what we get."

"You didn't want to go?"

"It's one of the best schools."

"But you'd have preferred elsewhere."

"Why would you say that?" he asks softly.

"Your expression. I don't know. Tell me about your family and your business."

Ryder does, and he spins charming tales out of everything. He's smooth and slick and weirdly lacking in artifice, even when I know he's speaking by rote.

And through this, even though he gets looks from women who come in, I can't tell if he sees them, he's focused on me. Or should I say, he's doing what I asked.

As we call it a night at two am, I wonder what it would be like to have that focus on me with such intent behind it, but I know I'd never stand a chance.

It's seven a.m. and I don't expect Ryder to be up, but he is. He's dressed and looking far perkier than I feel after a late night and a few more drinks than I usually have. I've gone extra professional today with my suit and pulled back hair and the way he looks at me makes me think he knows it's some kind of armor.

He stands in the doorway of his loft in TriBeCa with two cups and he says, "I'd ask you in, but you look dressed to murder the day."

"Shall we?" I ignore his comment. "Time's wasting."

"No store is open, Perry," he says, handing me a sleek to-go cup made of darkly brushed metal-finish. The coffee smells like heaven.

I take a sip. It tastes better than heaven. "This one is. I've a car waiting."

We drive across town to East Fortieth, just off Fifth Ave, and Ryder's dark head is bent over his phone as he sends out whatever he's sending on his phone. It looks like texts and emails, probably to do with work.

He doesn't say a word as I lead him out on the already busy street—people have places to go and deals to wield. The door is non-descript, just a sign on it that says Harold Daley's Custom. I buzz and it opens and we step into another era.

Custom-made suits, ones where every detail is considered, is an art, and this cool, quiet store with the dark wooden floorboards and sparse fittings is from another world.

Harold Daley is the best, and he dresses CEOs, presidents, celebrities, and the rich.

"Harry!" Ryder grins at the graying man in the sharp suit, who slaps him on the shoulder like an old friend. "It's been a while."

"A month." Harold looks from Ryder to me and back again. "Topping up? I've some styles and fabrics you'll love—"

"Actually," I say, "Ryder's here for a makeover…"

I look at him as we step out of the store. Ryder has a new wardrobe coming, and fast. One of the beautiful things with Harold is he can work as slow or quickly as a client can pay, and as Ryder's one of his best customers and can pay, we'll have his new wardrobe by Monday morning.

"Well?"

"That wasn't as bad as I thought it would be."

"Harold was out of specialty cages and leashes—"

"Leashes? I didn't know you were kinky. Tell me more."

"—so the suits had to do. I figured no one's going to believe you showing about town in a regular suit, even if it's made to order. But something with a touch of Ryder flair without the…erm flair works. Conservative but you."

He smiles. "I'm not sure whether I should be insulted or flattered."

"Settle for a bit of both," I say.

My phone buzzes and I dig it out of my pocket and click on the alert I've set up for anything Ryder related. All goodwill disintegrates as I read.

"I'd ask but your face is telling me it's not good."

"Is anything to do with you good?"

"I haven't done anything. I haven't had time."

I hand him my phone. "You have at some point. Another scandal?"

"Elliot—"

"No." I turn and glare. The article is every single reason why it's a bad idea I'm working for a guy I'll crush on for his looks. Hell, I can already feel the lust in my blood. I'm not sure who I'm disgusted with more. Me for being so horribly shallow, or him for being, well...him. "This one says you are her secret lover. Emphasis on are. Every single thing there is believable. You going to tell me I'm wrong?"

Chapter Five

RYDER

"Come on. I've never met her in my life."

I shouldn't be pissed off, but I am. Secret lover? Jesus. And Elliot actually believes this shit? Problem is I don't know how to explain my way out of this and not make myself sound like a giant douche.

Say I wouldn't sleep with the woman in the photo? I look like a douche. Explain that having a secret lover means a relationship? Douche.

So I don't explain a thing. Elliot can believe me or not. I have no reason to lie, so I say that. "This is just someone riding on the coattails of the other scandal. There's no reason to lie to you. I hired you to fix things for me. I'm not into hiding anything."

"I'll see what I can do and get this to go away. In the meantime, you now also don't do anything outside of work without me knowing. Is that clear?"

"Like glass."

"Good. I think we should come up with an itinerary—"

"Excuse me?" I call a car on my phone and give her my most neutral look. "I'm not a child."

"You want to change or at least appear to change, or what?"

It takes less than a minute for one of the Sinclair town cars to pull smoothly up to the curb and I open the door and gesture for her to get it. She's tall, so she doesn't have to lift her chin too far to meet my gaze. And hers is positively straight from the darkest period of the ice age.

I don't answer and it's a silent battle of wills. Normally, I'd go the charm route, a little smooth talking, compliments, warm glances. She doesn't like those and I'm not here to seduce her—whether it be out of her panties or me into her good books. So I wait. Behind us horns honk and people scream abuse as they want the parking spot, which is a coveted thing in this city.

"What I want is for you to get in the fucking car."

She's about to say something, but Elliot shakes her head instead and gets in and I take a moment to admire her ass as she does so. Her outfit doesn't do it justice, but the way her trousers stretch across it does.

I follow and clip my seatbelt on. Then I tap my fingers against the door's armrest. "I don't need an itinerary. This isn't political, this isn't even me trying to win the favor of the public—"

"No, but you're trying to win favor and prove you've changed, so to do that, you have to. Appearance wise and behavioral. If it was going to be easy for you, you wouldn't have hired me, Ryder."

"You got that right. But I don't need an itinerary. My life is ruled by that bullshit enough."

Her glance is long and thoughtful and she crosses those long legs. Because even in the trousers, her unflattering trousers, they're definitely the mile-long type of leg. "Structure, Ryder, is important here. It'll keep you out of trouble and your life ordered."

"Order is the bane of the gods."

Her mouth twitches a little as she clearly tries not to smile. "I'm not sure that's true."

"Well," I say darkly as the world of Manhattan shifts past us in the window of the car as we make our way to SoHo. I'm assuming she'll want to be at her office. "It should be."

"I'm not the enemy. And all my clients have an itinerary. It helps."

"Thing is, I have meetings that pop up, events. There are impromptu meals and drinks that are basically meetings in disguise. Many deals are lost or made over a drink or three."

"And in a strip club, no doubt," she mutters. "Which are off your schedule."

I open my mouth to say I don't go to places like that, but it's a lie. I joke about them with my brothers, but there are plenty out there who want places like that, and I go when I have to. There's an underlying sleaze to many, and there's also an honesty. Again, it's not something I'm about to say to this woman.

"You're in luck. I don't have anything like that penciled in on my dance card."

This time she does smile. "Or high class places where the waitstaff are barely clad."

"Now you're trying to ruin my life."

"Four weeks, Ryder. I'm sure you can manage." She pulls out her phone and mine pings a few seconds later. "Go through that. Places to keep away from, places you can go."

I look at my phone and shake my head. Her list is long. "Half the board of Sinclair's go to these places."

"Half the board isn't trying to keep Sinclair's within their namesake family's grasp."

"If it's fine with you," I say with heaping amounts of sarcasm, as if she hadn't made a salient point, "I have a whole bunch of meetings today—"

"Wear your most conservative suit."

"—and then I have to meet my brother and then go home."

We pull up outside her office, double parking on Prince Street, and she opens the door and gets out. Then she turns and bends to look at me. "Report in after."

As she slams the door and disappears into the building, I'm unsure whether she's serious, but I find myself smiling.

"You walk and talk like Ryder," Kingston drawls, "but the way you dress and who you were in there...have you been body snatched?"

I give him my filthiest look as I pull at the most boring tie I own. I look like a banker.

We've just come out of my fourth meeting of the day. My actual business where I make my money—as in mine and not family—was conducted before that redheaded Elliot demon with the intriguing mouth, terrible suit, and long legs turned up at my door. Then I had meetings for that.

The rest of my day's been spent on business here and there and finally this meeting with the board. It seemed regular enough, but I know our mother and she watched like an evil hawk. I'm leaving with Kingston; the others are gone already for their various duties before we meet about this whole thing.

"Ryder?"

I stop as my mother's voice holds a certain tone and Kingston slaps me on the back. "Meet you at Hud and Scarlett's."

"Asshole. Turncoat. Benedict Arnold of the real estate world."

He just waves a hand and saunters out of the Madison Ave office building that's been in the family for a couple of generations.

"Mother," I say, giving her my most charming smile, one she refuses to be charmed by. "You bellowed?"

"You haven't changed that much, even if you're dressed up."

I bite down on a sigh. Of course, Elliot's right in the clothes she went for. But me, not. This is pure not. But I keep this suit for funerals, court cases when and if they happen and...well, this.

"You're taking a huge interest." My gaze flickers to the door where Jenson stands, on his phone, making it clear he's not looking, which says he's paying attention.

She purses her lips. "I always take an interest in family business."

"A little closer than usual, I'd say."

"Ryder, everyone saw all that stuff today. The board won't say it, but they're not happy." She draws in a breath and glances at Jenson, then back to me. "I'm going to be a bigger part than usual in this."

I narrow my eyes. "What's your interest?"

"You."

"What is your real part in all this, mother?"

She smiles sweetly. "It's in that word. I want to make sure things are done right by my sons and your scandals haven't helped. The company could be lost, Ryder, if you don't clean up your act. Your father built that clause in to make sure you flew right. And...and I shouldn't be telling you this, but there will be four meetings of the board. The last one is where the decision is made.

If you have the capability to truly change. Which is why I'm there. I know you best. I'll know. And I can't go easy on you."

My mother rises up and kisses my cheek. "I have faith. So don't let me down."

And as she leaves with Jenson, I wonder what her agenda really is.

Because she's the one woman I can't hoodwink.

"Really?"

My so-called siblings grin. I'm with their better halves who look both embarrassed and annoyed.

"What?" Hudson looks at the board and at me. "Too ornate?"

"No, it's fine. Top quality chalk. Maybe if we got him some strippers to carry it..." Mag says, earning an elbow to the ribs from Zoey. "Ow."

I point at Hud. "You've changed." Then at Mag. "You haven't."

"Here," says Scarlett. "Have a drink. It'll cheer you up. I'm on your side."

"Me too."

I throw myself in a seat and take the proffered drink and glare at the chalkboard. "You're actually taking bets?"

"Well, you look like a terrible banker, but you also apparently have a secret lover, so I'm saying the odds are on our sides." Kingston grins. "I want the money."

"You're betting on the least amount of time."

"I know you, Ry."

The rest join in and they give me hell. But my outrage, while real, is only half there. Along with my attention. My mind keeps going back to the mouthy redhead.

"It's going to be boring," says the evil Magnus.

"But it's four weeks," I point out. "I can stand being bored that long."

"No," says King, "you can't. You can barely stand being bored for four minutes. The money is all mine. Double or nothing, guys."

He's right. I hate being bored. Who doesn't hate that? I like stimulation, interesting things and this should be heading right into the most boring four weeks of my life, but... I don't know. There's something about Elliot that says I won't be bored in the slightest.

And it's got nothing to do with the fact she doesn't like me. Okay, she'll warm to me, but she's not about to eat out of my hand, even if I turned on the Ryder charm. That interests me. Almost as much as the fact she's going to make sure I save the company and get my Sinclair jewel.

Eye on the prize.

When my phone buzzes with a message from an old college buddy who wants to meet for a drink and discuss a real estate opportunity, I text back where.

Eye on the prize. I can do this.

I agree to meet up in the Meat Packing district, the area full of high-end designer stores and places to be seen. The drinks and conversation are about what I expect when I meet Jaden. I'm not interested in the deal, and it's nice enough to meet up with someone I don't have to impress, but I stay on my best behavior. I even turn down a proposition and make Jaden's night by turning one into his.

I'm feeling good when I leave.

Right up to the moment I'm grabbed by someone. I get an impression of platinum blonde hair and a familiar, strong perfume.

"Lacey—"

That's all I manage before she kisses me and the world lights up in a series of flashes.

Oh fuck.

This is bad.

Chapter Six

ELLIOT

"Oh, hell no."

I glare at my phone. At the pictures on it that come with the stupid alert.

Double hell and double no and everything else.

Of course, the very hot, the very sexy, the very beautiful man whore that is Ryder Sinclair would revisit the scene of the crime. I'd just stupidly hoped he'd take longer than a handful of hours after I'd left him.

I'd given him the instructions on how to dress. I'd told him not to get into trouble, especially after the article over the woman claiming to be his secret lover, and now this?

Here I am, working late into the hours of the morning, putting too much time and effort into his contract, knowing one month isn't that long, and he does this.

I close my eyes as something hot and white and shameful streaks through me.

Yeah, I've also been sitting here, thinking about that sensuous mouth of his, those lips on me, those hands, his tongue on my skin.

Thinking might be too formal a word.

I'm an idiot.

That bullshit aside, the asshole's actively sabotaging this.

Fury, dark and sharp edged sweeps through me and I shove my notes into my bag, feet into the lime green running shoes I wear whenever I attempt such a thing, but usually just to jog down to the corner store in the middle of the night when I realize I need food, grab my coat, and head out the door.

I'm about to be that gorgeous, sexy, man whore's reckoning.

It takes him a while to answer his door.

For a long moment, he stares at me and I stare back, unable to breathe.

I'm pretty sure we're staring at each other for entirely different reasons.

He's staring at me out of surprise and sleep and probably a nugget of guilt if he's capable of such things.

And me?

Lust. Pure lust.

He's clad only in a pair of boxer shorts in black and he looks better than I could have imagined. Better than I thought.

Those long, lean muscular legs, narrow hips—I'm not even going to let myself focus on the substantial bulge of his junk, because hey, maybe he's a shower not a grower, but I doubt it—the washboard abs and broad chest. And on his arm is the tattoo that winds, a vine with thorns and intricate skeletons and flowers up his flesh from above the wrist to where it seems to disappear over his shoulder.

That's all I see, because he pulls on a sweater that's in his other hand and crosses his arms over his chest as the sleep disappears and annoyed curiosity remains.

"What are you doing here, and how did you find me?" he asks.

"I was here this morning, idiot," I say, not bothering to hide the bite in my voice as I look about the vast foyer that I can see beyond him. "Where is she?"

"Who?"

I narrow my eyes and hit him with my stare. "I don't have time for games, Ryder."

"I don't have time for banshees turning up at ungodly hours like some forgotten wife."

"Where is she? The photos are everywhere."

He doesn't look surprised. Why would he? He was there.

Ryder sighs. "I'm alone."

"That was fast."

He rubs a hand over his face. "I'll ignore the insult, Elliot. On account of the hour at hand. And no one other than you has been here, okay?"

"I'm meant to believe that?"

Ryder grabs my arm, and even through the coat I'm wearing, I can feel the heat of him, the bite of his touch, an awareness as he drags me in and kicks the heavy metal door shut. He lets me go and locks it. "No need to entertain half of New York."

"Any more than you already have."

He just looks at me and turns, striding off down the open space of the foyer before turning right into what must be his living room. I follow.

The old industrial space is open with cleverly placed half walls and glass to section it while keeping the openness. The metal and exposed beams are a nod to its previous life, but everything in here is beautifully thought out and placed.

He has the money for the best decorators around.

There's a wide, winding staircase leading up to the next level, but he ignores that and gestures to a mid-Century sofa in red.

"I didn't do anything, okay?"

"Photographic evidence seems to prove otherwise." I hold up my phone. "As I said, the photos are everywhere. And Red Light? Really? It's a high-end meat market in the aptly named district."

"It's also a bar where people go for drinks."

"Celebrities, the rich." I glare and he glares back. "The kind of rich you're trying to pretend not to be."

"I went out for a fucking drink with a friend."

"Who's married."

"I'm not sure that's the real situation with Lacey and whatever his name is, but that's not my problem." He stops, marches over to a wet bar, pours a drink, looks at it, and then at me. "Okay, it's my problem, but I didn't do anything."

"And yet you chose there for a meet up."

"Not," he says, stalking back to the middle of the room, leaving the drink behind, "with her. A friend. Male. College friend who wanted to meet up, talk about a deal I'm not interested in. Not after I heard it."

"Offices. Daylight. Lunch. You know, the things I set out for you."

"I'm not your performing monkey."

"You hired me so I could make you into what you're not." I look at the photo on my phone of the passionate make out. His hands are on her face and it says they're about to get down and dirty right there. "I ask again, what's this?"

He jabs a finger at my phone. "That is me trying to get her off me. She stuck her tongue in my mouth, not the other way around."

"You—"

"And if you look, I'm stopping it. I'm pushing her away, not pulling her into me. I didn't enjoy it. I didn't ask for it. I stopped it. Immediately. Jesus." He gives me a disgusted look. "I don't like being mauled against my will."

"No one does."

Ryder nods. "That was her, not me. and she bought the fucking cameras. I'm innocent here."

And weirdly, I believe him. He looks so pissed off and out of sorts that I believe him. I'm most definitely a fool. Because only a fool would do that. By his own admission, he's a fuck up in this department. He hired me, not the other way around and here I am, trying not to ogle all that glorious man flesh that's suddenly very personal and keep an even and objective head about me.

Just because he's charming and has a smile that does things to a female, or eyes that can make a polar ice cap melt, doesn't mean he's innocent. At all.

And it makes everything way more difficult.

I breathe out, trying to find room to think.

"You just made my job harder," I say.

"How?"

"By being...you. This is totally you, not caring about anyone else, by just wanting to have a good time. For enjoying it."

"So I make your job harder for liking to have a good time—which I wasn't by the way—and enjoying women, which is something I'll always enjoy, Elliot."

"No," I answer, clear and concise, "because you flagrantly went and flouted my rules and guidelines. You deliberately went to a place where the paps love to go. Where celebs love to go. You went there because you knew it would cause a stir."

"Bullshit." He shoves his too-long, softly curling, sleep tousled hair back. "Why would I go and sabotage something I actively want?"

"You just told me how much you enjoy women."

"I do. But I didn't plan that."

"Maybe," I say, "You did."

"And why would I do that?" His voice has turned dark and low and deadly, and it's as electrifying as it is thrilling.

"I don't know. Maybe this is how you get your rocks off."

"I'm telling you, I didn't kiss her. I didn't ask her there. And I didn't plan anything."

"And?"

"*And*? Do you believe me?

"Not on your life, fuck boy."

His eyes narrow, then glitter with intent, like a hunter who's just spotted his prey. I swallow and back away.

He follows. "Damned either way with you, is that it?"

I'm playing with fire. I know that, and I can't stop. "You were born damned. Give me one reason why I should believe you."

"Because, Elliot, I don't operate that way."

"What way?"

"The forceful way. The whatever way you think I do. Like luring a woman I'm keeping away from to meet me and attacking her in public. In front of the cameras. If I wanted her, she'd be here and you wouldn't know it. If I wanted a woman, I don't need to go that route."

"Oh, you have super powers, is that it?"

"No. I'm just very good at seduction." Suddenly he smiles and the charm is focused in on me.

Right now, I'm looking like a...what did he say? A banshee. I'm in lime green running shoes, Godzilla pajama pants and an oversize pastel pink Sparkle Warrior Princess T-shirt, courtesy of my niece. In short, I look a fright, and he's looking at me like I'm the most delicious thing he's ever seen and I don't care it's a game, I don't care about anything but that look and the man who owns it.

I'm in his sights, and he comes toward me, slow and deliberate. The air crackles. He's so close, so close I can see the shots of copper striations in his melting chocolate eyes. Flame is there, too, as he caresses me with his gaze and it licks inside me, slow and sensuous.

Ryder slides that gaze slowly over my face to linger on my mouth. My breath is uneven, and every slam of my heart is pure and unadulterated need for him.

He leans in, fingers touching me, setting me alight. It's not high combustion. This is more insidious, this setting alight. It's soft and warm and a different kind of flame.

I'm singing where he draws a path, and that gorgeous mouth comes in close, like he wants to kiss me.

"Elliot..."

The soft sound of my name does indecent things to me. And the longing and promises there make my sex throb.

My eyes flutter shut and his breath heats along my skin to my ear. "You think I need to get all forceful in public? And do you think, if I was messing with someone else, I'd hit on you like this? Or do you think I need to lie?"

I snap out of it at his word. I glare at him. "You'd never hit on me."

"Then," he says, keeping that same soft and seductive tone, "what was that?"

"You teaching me a lesson."

I suck in air and twist away, digging in my bag for my notebook and pen. I almost forgot it was there, on my shoulder.

"Why do you think I wouldn't hit on you?"

"Have you seen me?"

"I'm pretty fucking sure I'm looking at you right now."

I perch on the red sofa. "Let's say I believe you—"

"No. Why do you think I wouldn't? I like women."

"You like certain women."

He smiles but there's a curiosity in his gaze and that heat and smoke and fire is shut away. "I'm equal opportunity when it comes to females."

I don't know what that means and so I just repeat, "You were teaching me a lesson. Consider it made. Now, can we do some triage here? I'd like to get to sleep."

"Yeah, okay." But I get the feeling he doesn't want to let go of the conversation, and he's not going to forget it. Does the man need to conquer every woman? Damn him.

Ryder takes the seat opposite. It's a black matching chair to the sofa and I smooth the notebook open and don't look at him. It seems safe that way.

I start making notes as I talk. "One of the things I need you to be aware of is body language, word choices, tone—"

"That's more than one."

"You need to do this when you think no one is looking, because someone always is. And alone with someone you don't know well means no witnesses."

I'm going to have a full day tomorrow handling the fall out and twisting it to what we need. But two things so close together can work in my favor. No one's accusing him of anything untoward, it's more coattail riding, and I can deal with that.

"Yeah, tell me something new."

"I'm telling you because I have to keep drumming it in, Ryder. You need to play nice, and you also need not to play with anyone of the female persuasion."

"I'm not."

A part of me wants to mention yours truly, but I stop myself. I need to get out of here, and I have an idea forming. I stand. "Okay. I'm going to make some calls first thing, and you are going to go about your day in your boring suit. You have an event tomorrow, right?"

He stands, too. "Yes."

"Good." I pack everything up. "You owe me more money."

"You're already getting a small fortune." He doesn't seem particularly bothered.

"Now it's going to be a bigger one." I nod at him. "The event?"

"What about it?"

"Send me all the relevant details." I smile. "Be prepared."

"Why does that sound ominous?"

"It isn't," I say. "You'll be meeting your new life partner for the next four weeks."

Chapter Seven

RYDER

All day long, Elliot's parting words have haunted me.

Life partner?

What the fuck does that mean?

Is she suddenly going to try and spin it that I secretly bat for the other team? It's an interesting concept, if so, and I know plenty of gay men and women, none of whom fit into any stereotype, but I'm not exactly sure if anyone would buy it. Even for four weeks.

Still, I'm on the Bowery, at the cutting edge gallery where Sinclairs, in conjunction with one of the foundations Magnus set up to show he had heart, and that we've all donated heavily to, is having an event. An art show and auction that the hefty ticket price along with donations will go to doing good.

And I'm looking out for this life partner, as well as aware I'm being watched.

One thing is I'm not the focus of the local and national rags and blogs. I've another scandal that has nothing to do with me—thank goodness—to thank for that.

I catch my mother's eye and she raises a glass of champagne to me. I offer a tight smile.

Her gaze shifts, her eyebrows rise, and I follow.

Oh. My.

The woman is tall with Rita Hayworth hair, now it's down, and that body she hides beneath the wrong clothes is to die for. Curves and full and with that mouth painted siren red, Elliot Perry is a knockout.

It's not even the looks, it's her attitude.

And she's heading straight for me.

The lick of lust dies as annoyance rises up instead. She doesn't trust me, even here, and the hot shimmery black dress that skims those hot curves clings and offers me a view of cleavage I could lose myself in. Or not. I'm ready to battle.

She's so close now that the effect of hot and confident siren is slammed down to the ground by the slight self-consciousness in her eyes. It should ruin it. It doesn't. It gives it earthiness. Another layer. Like I'm seeing a secret. And that's hot all over again.

Does this fucking place come with cold showers?

Elliot stops in front of me. "Ryder."

"Wha—"

She slaps me.

Whatever I was going to ask is lost in the shock.

The slap doesn't hurt; she cups her hand in such a way it makes a sound but doesn't do anything more than send a slight jolt through me that's almost pleasing. Well, color me all sorts of kink I apparently didn't know about.

I grab her, sliding and arm around her waist and catching her hand as she raises it again. "What the fuck, Elliot?" I whisper.

"Just make this real."

"That was real."

Her gaze is both pleading and irritated. "I didn't hurt you."

"Maybe I'm sensitive."

"And maybe you're a man baby."

I offer a small, low smile. "A man baby fuck boy? Now that's a combination."

She goes to pull away, but I tighten my grip to stop her, even though I don't need to. Because her attempt to get away is for show. I'm not that dazzled by her Cinderella transformation to not grasp that. But I want to know what's up her non-existent sleeves. "Ryder, you're all over the papers."

A flash goes off. "And I'm about to be again. This time starring you in the scandal."

"I lead a very upstanding life!"

"I'm sure you do."

Her eyes narrow and I've insulted her, but I'm not sure how. She isn't about to be the type with skeletons anywhere and she isn't a fame and fortune seeker.

"Yes," she says with a healthy amount of bitterness, "and you should be glad. Now follow my lead. I'm saving your ungrateful ass. Right now you're explaining Lacey kissed you last night—"

"Blah," I say. "Blah, blah with added blah. Happy?"

"You have a reputation where the tarnish goes so deep it's going to take my sparkly one to help you."

"So we're dating now?"

"Would that be so hard to believe?" Her intriguing mouth curls up in a smile that's sweet and sarcastic and vulnerable. "If I said, yes, we are dating."

"What's this?" My mother is there, eyes big, expression cool as she takes us in. "Dating?"

I expect Elliot to fall apart, flounder, but she doesn't.

"You must be Faye Sinclair," Elliot says, pulling her wrist from my light grip. "So pleased to meet you. I'm—"

"Mother, this is my girlfriend, Elliot Perry."

I get a sharp look from both of them. Like I'd just announced I'm secretly a serial killer. Usually I'm way smoother than this, smoother than silk. But Elliot has a way about her. I don't even know if she was planning on going this way, but hey, I might as well have some fun since I don't exactly have any other outlets for the next few weeks.

"Girlfriend? You, Ryder? She looks out of your league." Then she smiles up at Elliot. "He's a good boy, but you could do better."

I narrow my eyes at my mother and grip Elliot's waist a little harder and I try not to think how good she feels beneath my palm, how warm and alive and vital.

"He's on a thin rope right now. Although I can't hold him too accountable for things that happened before we met. Can you believe he wanted to hire my PR company?"

"He could use it." Amusement plays over my mother's face.

"But he just finished explaining how that woman kissed him last night."

"One thing he isn't, is a liar."

"I am here," I say.

They both ignore me. "Perry? Don't tell me you're related to the Cape Cod Perry's. Anastasia?"

"That's my mother," Elliot says.

And my mother is off, launching into how she knows Elliot's mother through a network of friends—not close, but they move in similar circles. Then she asks Elliot about various people and it hits me she is related to them. Including an ex-quarterback who owns a team, and a model that I haven't had the…er…pleasure of meeting.

But I'm looking at Elliot in a different light. Not because she comes from money—I do, too. It's how she doesn't seem to come from money. From the sound of it, her family is sprawling and she's in the middle. I study her.

Elliot deflects with the kind of mastery that makes her the perfect mirror. Right now it's a little deliberate, but I can't shake the feeling it's inherent in her, like she lets the rest shine.

After they finish chatting, my mother takes us around and she does Elliot's work by letting it be known we're together. Kingston is there and he just raises a brow at me, and the way he slides his gaze over Elliot annoys me on a level I don't understand.

For some reason I don't go over, and when my mother is distracted, I pull Elliot to a corner and shove a glass of champagne in her hand and lean in. "Was that your plan?"

"My plan was to save you from yourself. Hence the slap. It also felt good."

I take the champagne I just gave her and swallow some down, before giving it back. "Yeah? It didn't hurt."

She looks at me, then at the glass, and turns it from where I drank from and then takes a delicate sip. I grab it again.

"It wasn't meant to, Ryder. But it still felt good. The symbolism."

I point the champagne at her. "I should fire you."

"You should. But then you'd be without all those pretty little things you want, like the Sinclair jewels. And your family company."

"It might be worth it."

She smiles. "Then I'll make everything come back and bite you hard on the ass. And I'll sharpen its teeth first." She shrugs. "I've put a lot of effort into you the past couple of days. Don't fight the gift horse."

"Why are you my fake girlfriend?"

"That was you taking my bait. This is strategic, Ryder," Elliot says, sliding a hand down the buttons of my dress shirt. The move is slightly disconcerting and I don't know why. Her touch is something that slides down beneath the skin to nestle warm against my bones.

"How so?"

"I slap you like an outraged girlfriend, we have words. Your mother spreads the seed of your reform with who you're dating. There are photos of it, and...the latest scandal? This helps put the final nail in that disappearing. A woman was mad you didn't want her back. You went home alone, and I turned up so if someone was watching, it all plays out in your hands."

"So you believe me now?"

She shrugs again and takes the champagne back from me. "She was mad. Like I said."

"Okay." I'm not sure I believe her.

But she looks divine, and someone I'm happy to have on my arm. If I'm a little turned on, well, who could blame me? It's been a while—for me—and she looks delicious. More than that, she's intriguing and this time I'm not talking about just her mouth.

"Besides." Elliot stares down into what's left of the champagne. "No one's going to believe you went for me for the usual reasons. It'll be seen as a step into maturity, into the role you want to inhabit."

I laugh.

"Just pretend."

"First, no one's going to believe I'm that mature."

"I know what I look like, Ryder. No need to keep going." She checks her watch. "We should get out of here—"

"Wait." I take her arm and she stops right before she starts to spin away.

Elliot sounds smooth, classy, untouchable, but I can't shake the feeling I insulted her.

"You look good tonight. Like someone I might go for."

"Ryder."

Her voice is a warning I ignore. I can get out of any situation, and this is a no brainer. She looks pretty under her usual severe hair and clothes. "I just meant you look pretty. You should wear your hair like that more often."

"And smile?"

"Well..." I stop. "That's a trick question."

"No, it isn't. I'm talking commonsense."

I breathe out. "There are beautiful women who'd kill for me to say that."

"That it's a trick question?"

"That they look pretty." She stiffens and I know immediately that was the wrong thing to say. Shit.

"We should go."

"Elliot." I catch her free hand and draw her closer. "It was meant to be a compliment."

"Implying the rest of the time I'm ugly?" Her cheeks flush high. "I'm not fishing for compliments. I don't need them or your practiced words."

"I don't practice that shit."

"I should go."

"All I meant," I say, having another go, "is most women like it. That's all. And I do not for the life of me know where I'm going wrong. Are you an alien?"

But Elliot doesn't smile at my joke. Instead, she just presses her lips together a moment, then finishes the champagne. "Maybe you should try to talk to women like they're people, not playthings."

"I do both." I stop. "That came out wrong."

"No, Ryder," she says after a long beat, "I think it just might have been one of the most honest things you've said all night." Elliot hands me the empty glass and I hand it to a passing waiter with a tray. "Speaking of night. It's late, I should go."

I still have her hand and I pull her into me, just that little bit closer and she smells like gardenias. Clean and pure with a hint of earthiness that's somehow erotic beneath it. "Stay. What if I get into trouble?"

"I think you can manage an art show."

"They're dangerous. Doubly so when they're also fundraisers. Besides, they bring out creatures like that." I gesture with my head at an old dowager who's basically a walking skeleton with giant bakelite vintage glasses and jewelry that had to be worth a cool quarter million.

I think she's also wearing a bright pink fluffy dog as a hat.

"You know who that is?"

"No." I raise a brow. "Should I?"

"So you're not after her for her money, just her looks. That's Madame Cohen-Paisley."

"I'm only after her for her sex appeal and beauty." I smile at Elliot. "C'mon, Perry, stay. Save me and have some fun."

She looks around and a slow grin blooms on that intriguing mouth. "Only because I don't think any of these people will be safe."

And for the next hour we study the art, have conversations with people we've made up histories for, and I honestly don't know if I've ever had such a good time at one of these things.

Certainly not with my clothes on.

Definitely not without getting into trouble.

Absolutely not with someone I'm not into.

"You see?" I say to Elliot, "these stodgy people are what I'm rebelling against."

She snorts laughter. "You're not a rebel, Sinclair. What you are, is a sad man in need of help."

"Oh, God. You're going to lecture me?"

"Me? Never. I'm just pointing out you have problems. You're not a rebel. You're someone whose dick needs a support group. And," she says, shooting me the kind of severe look a sadistic boarding school nun would salivate over, "before you say it, not that kind of support group, one where your dick gets a helping hand or something else."

I wait because she looks so proper but this is some fucked up shit she's saying and I'm really beginning to like her.

"No, Sinclair, you need the rehabilitation and abstinence kind of support group."

"No whipping?"

She looks me up and down, and fuck if she doesn't have one of the best poker faces I've ever seen. "Absolutely not. Someone as far gone as you would probably enjoy that."

"You're no fun."

"Welcome to relationships 101." She glances at a slender watch on her wrist. "I should go."

"We should go."

I don't give her a chance to say otherwise. I get our coats and start to lead her outside when I spot the paparazzi, ready to get whatever shots of whoever is in there. So I decide to give them a show.

"Work with me, Elliot."

And I slide her coat on, straighten the collar and before she knows what I'm doing, before I can second guess myself, I pull her up against me and kiss her.

Chapter Eight

ELLIOT

It's like heaven has exploded inside me. Pleasure and unexpected tenderness, and then a deep flame straight from hell. Delicious, decadent, and wild.

Ryder Sinclair's mouth is on mine and it's perfection. I gasp and his tongue slides along my lip, into my mouth, and thought simply stops.

It's just pure sensation.

I cling to him, my entire body a flickering flame of need and desire and delight. He tastes like champagne and a sweet, spiced something that's deep and dark like a tryst and I want more.

He pulls back, mouth brushing mine with a lingering, trembling note of such tenderness I get instantly why women don't hold grudges against him for his love and leave ways. I completely understand why they fall over themselves to just have him look at them or kiss them like that. And if he can kiss, then oh, fuck, what the hell can he do with sex?

There's a magic to him and I can see it, taste it, feel it. His breath is warm and slightly uneven on my damp lips, and he whispers my name.

"Elliot..."

He hasn't let me go and he's about to say something else when everything lights up bright white.

"Shit. I almost forgot," he mutters.

I come back to the Earth with a bang. In all that, I'd forgotten I'd orchestrated the paps, and as Ryder locks my gaze with his, I know that's why he kissed me. He saw them and took the opportunity.

I'd just planned to walk out with him, holding him close, maybe get him to bend his head to mine like we spoke loving words to each other, but that... I can't even be mad at him for kissing me.

There's a slightly shocked light in his eyes, but I put it down to the flash of the cameras.

I smile. "You did good, kid," I say, tugging him along to the sleek black car that's pulled up to us.

Some of the paps are shouting to him, but Ryder ignores them and bundles us into the car.

He closes the door on the noise as slides a glance my way as he dances his fingers along the sleeve of my coat.

"I didn't mean to kiss you," he says, making my heart stutter in my chest.

"Listen—"

"I mean I did. Mean to kiss you. I just didn't think it would go that far." He takes his hand back and rests it on his thigh. "I'll stop before I get myself into trouble."

"Turning a new leaf?"

Ryder laughs and shakes his head. "I stole a kiss."

"I'll write about it in my bright pink diary."

"Not lime green to match your sneakers? Or Godzilla themed? Or whatever that monstrosity of a T-shirt was you wore?"

"You're not funny, Ryder."

He bumps my shoulder with his and a small little thrill races along my veins. "You like me."

I do. That's the problem. "I don't."

"I'm growing on you."

"Like a fungus?"

"A handsome fungus," he says so seriously that I burst out laughing. "I was thinking we shouldn't call it a night."

I study him a long moment. "I know it's been a second for you and you've just entered into your first dry spell, but I'm not a consolation prize."

"Hardly. But I wouldn't go home. Not if I was dressed up."

"You're pretending to turn a new leaf. You're pretending you're mature and responsible."

"Yes," he says, shifting to look at me, "but there's that and there's being so out of character. Besides, what better way to show a new me than taking my newly appointed girl out on the town?"

I shouldn't do it. I know that. But he has a point. One that makes sense. One that's actually smart. And, I'm dressed up.

"Okay, but I pick."

"Deal."

The little club we go to is in the labyrinth-like streets of the village, the curved Commerce Street, right off the tangle where Manhattan's grid stops, and the place is down an unassuming flight of steps.

"Are you taking me to some kind of dungeon?"

The humor in his voice makes me smile as I push open the door. "Don't get your hopes up."

"Me? Never."

Ryder's looking about with a gleam in his eye and no doubt he's enjoying all the eye candy. And inside I'm struggling to hold myself together, to nail myself to solid ground because, holy damn, Ryder kissed me.

The thought won't go away.

And the senses memory?

It zooms and flirts and swoops inside me. I can still feel his mouth on mine. The erotic slide of his tongue. The heat and wetness and the masterful concerto he can create with a kiss.

I can still feel his hands on me as he took my lips with his.

And he only did it to further his agenda, which is what I'm here for.

He leads us through the elegant young things, and the elegant older things, too. People are dressed up, and there to be seen, but also just do their thing.

This place is a little jazzy, a little quirky, and lacking in sleaze. I like it, but more importantly, I figured it would be somewhere that would fit Ryder 2.0.

We slide into a little booth and I can't help but notice his leg, long, firm, warm, is pressed against mine.

"What is this place?"

"A little bar. Not the kind you go to, but it's got that vibe without the sleaze."

Ryder raises a brow. "Interesting choice of words there, Perry."

"I just meant it's more...grown up."

"Yeah. I got that." The lights go up on a stage and there's a smattering of applause as a tuxedoed band takes the stage, and a woman with amber hair and a figure hugging dress starts to sing in a low voice.

Ryder's gaze is pinned to her. And that's not jealousy I feel. Not at all. Of course, he'd watch the most mesmerizing woman in the room. Her figure won't quit and she has oodles of talent. The sultry sexiness of love mourned in her song winds around the room and I study the cocktail menu. It's a dark place, with well placed low orangey lights. Even the stage is lit in such a way it doesn't disturb the vibe of the place.

"The violet martini," he says.

I look up and he's watching me and no one else.

And it's hard to breathe.

There's a light in his gaze that ignites me. I'm sure it's something he doesn't think about, just uses. But it's like he can see right down into me, down into my secret self, where I'm beautiful. Because that's how he looks at me. Like I'm that. Like he likes what he sees. Like he wants it.

"You've been here before? And don't look at me like that."

"No. I can read, though. It's a skill, what can I say? One of the many I possess." Ryder pauses. "And what way?"

"Like you..." I trail off. I don't want to say like your latest conquest. That's laughable and I don't want Ryder Sinclair to laugh at me in that way. "Like you're making the look part of the act."

He slides his fingers over mine. "Part of the act? That this is a date?"

"Yes."

"It wouldn't be much of a date, fake or otherwise, if I didn't look at you like you fascinate me." He lowers his voice to thick, melted chocolate. The darkest kind. "Which you do."

I swallow. God, he's a dangerous man.

The waitress chooses that moment to arrive and ask what we'd like to drink. Ryder looks at me with a raised brow and I nod. "Two violet martinis, please."

And he hands her a black AmEx.

"I think we should strategize the next—"

"Perry." He takes my hand in his and rubs his thumb against my flesh, making me shiver and my thoughts scatter. "No more shop, okay?"

"Sinclair." I know I should pull my hand away, I know he's flirting on automatic, but it feels so good, I figure what's the harm in a few seconds more. "This is your dime, you know."

"It's a lot of my dimes. Do you want to be paid in dimes? We can do it, but it'll probably make life worth it. How about unmarked bills?"

"Do you ever take anything seriously?"

"Great sex, a beautiful woman who's fantastic company, making money, and my work. Did I mention sex?"

I pull my hand back to my side of the table just as the waitress reappears and her eyes widen at my move. I don't blame her. I must seem like a lunatic to snatch my hand away from such a beautiful man. She places the small black leather folder with the bill in it next to Ryder's hand and her fingers accidentally on purpose touch him.

He doesn't even notice, his gaze still on me, as he says thanks.

When she's gone, he adds, "I mean, you're the beautiful woman."

"I'm not beautiful."

He studies me for a long moment. "You don't like compliments. You don't like flirting. You don't like being the center of attention. What is it you like, Elliot?"

"I'm not the center of attention. I don't command it the way you do or half the people in here do."

"You did when you walked in to the event dressed like that."

I wrinkle my nose at him and glance away for a second. "Costume and bells and whistles."

"Or," he says, picking up his drink and taking a sip, "you let yourself shine a moment. Two sides to everything, Elliot."

He's flirting again, but I shift the conversation to the night we just had, and soon we're laughing over some of the silly conversations, some of the outfits of the mega rich who don't give a damn. Not long after, he starts telling me some of the things he did at college.

"You did not." I stare at him. I believe him, but I'm trying to imagine Ryder with pink hair.

He whips out his phone and drags up a photo and shows me.

I can't help it. I start laughing. He looks adorable, ridiculous, and young.

"That's so rude, Perry," he says. "It was for a good cause."

"No. You just told me you dyed your hair bright pink to win a bottle of Wild Turkey."

"As I said, I have a good cause. I despise Wild Turkey, but I was trying to impress a girl with it."

"Of course you were."

He nods sagely. "She's a fine woman, Rosalita. I think she was seventy then, and looked amazing. Also, she made the best damn poblano and roasted squash tamales I've ever had. I just wanted the recipe."

I give him a curious look and smile against my will. He'll take it and run because I've learned fast that's what he does. If this man was unattractive and a pauper, I've a feeling women would still hang off him because that's the super power he has.

He's charming, he's self-effacing, he makes you the center of the universe and he'd coax the underwear off a saint. And the man is funny.

"You can cook?"

"I've been known to dabble. But I'm no Rosalita."

"Ah, but did the whiskey work?"

He sighs and it's a theatrical sound. "Well, she said she'd keep feeding me, maybe teach me some things, but that recipe would have to be pried out of her cold, dead hands." He pauses. "She's still causing trouble in her little restaurant, so...no luck there."

Then Ryder smiles low. "Maybe we should go."

"I'm on the clock, remember? And you've got a time crunch."

"After."

Oh, Lord. After. It's so loaded, that word. "We'll see."

We won't. I know that. Because he'll be on to his pastures he likes. Fresh, full of beautiful women.

"I'm taking that as a yes," he says.

And as he smiles at me, a straight to the heart, screw armor and defenses and everything else smile, I realize my mistake in working with him.

This is a man a woman could fall for. Hard.

There are depths.

Layers.

And he's got a genuine core beneath the beauty and his charm and sex appeal and dangerous ways.

Ryder Sinclair.

I'm crushing on him. Oh, so hard I'm basically glittery dust and future hurt.

Because this gorgeous billionaire is a man that no woman, especially not one like me, should ever lose their head over.

He might not mean it. He probably won't ever notice.

But Ryder's a man who can destroy a heart without pausing.

Including mine.

Chapter Nine

Ryder

I'm actually having a great time.

The martinis are good, the violet adding a touch of something floral without tasting like those terrible mint things you can still buy for reasons known only to the gods themselves.

Elliot finishes her drink and I order another for us. "Go lightly," I warn, "this isn't your normal martini. It has Crème de Violette for the floral and vanilla notes, which are enhanced by the kick of Cutty Sark hundred proof that gives a chocolatey depth, and it's cut by lemon juice, and elevated by the honey syrup."

"You're reading the ingredients."

"True. But they used spiced honey, with a touch of black pepper and the hint of salt and complex lemon."

Her gaze is on me as her finger taps against the stem of her glass. She's got a little glow from the buzz of the booze and it only enhances her. I called her beautiful because women are beautiful. But she's not plain like I first thought. But I also don't think she's beautiful in that sense of the word.

There's something there that makes her way more interesting than beautiful or pretty or plain.

She's both confident and vulnerable. In command and deliberately tries to chameleon herself into whatever situation she's in, so she goes unseen. But once you see Elliot Perry, good luck unseeing her.

She's got a sweetness and she's prickly as fuck.

Sharp, too. I like her intelligence.

And maybe I've had one too many of these damn drinks. It's when they're blended so perfectly and they don't taste like booze that they get you.

"Yes?"

"That's the preserved lemon they use. And I bet they slide some into the lemon juice, too."

I don't want to go home. Sure, I love being out. I love meeting people, or I should say, women. I love what happens when I do go home, or to wherever it might be so I can give and take pleasure. But right now? I like being here. With Elliot.

Holy shit, I could spend time with her and not be trying to not imagine her naked. Not going there. I could do that, because I like spending actual time, clothes on, with her.

I also liked kissing her.

But kissing is an art that is always good.

That kiss, though... It had been spectacular.

Maybe because it was what it was. A lovely thing that had no agenda attached. Private agenda.

"Is this your way of telling me you wanted to be a bartender?"

I laugh. "Mixologist. No. But if you know how things work, then you get more from them."

"So that's why you're so good with women."

I'm really not sure what to say. She keeps blindsiding me with things that never blindsided me in the past.

I know she thinks I'm hot. But she also isn't interested in flirting. And she keeps taking things I say the wrong way. It's like I've stepped into a version of the world when I'm with her that I don't quite understand.

And that's a good thing. Because I need not to be sidetracked. I also think we're becoming friends. Which is both weird and good, and I know I can work with that.

Elliot glances at her watch then back at me. "I think we've stayed out long enough to make it look good. Let's call it a night."

Something like disappointment overtakes me, even though I nod.

Being with Elliot is fun. She's weird and cool and I can talk to her. I can talk to anyone, anytime, but this is different. Like there's a layer of something missing, making this easy, like we connect. It just is.

That keeps returning to me as I pay the final bill and we get our things and go.

The ease with her. The natural flow.

Elliot Perry is intriguing in more ways than one.

Out on the street, I turn to her. "We could walk."

"Are you offering to walk me home, Ryder?" she asks.

Am I? "Maybe you've just uncovered my secret—I'm a tightass with money."

"I don't think so. And did I say you'd be paying for the car?" She calls an Uber.

"Somehow I think I'll be doing that."

She laughs. "I'll be billing you."

"So, we should walk."

"Tell you what," Elliot says, looking me in the eye. At her height and in the heels she's wearing she's up there. And I like it. "We'll walk, but you wear my shoes."

I glance at her feet as a cold gust of wind pulls at us. "They'll never fit me, I'm afraid."

Just then a gold car pulls up. "Saved by the car service."

The driver is playing some Indian rap, I think. The car moves slow, as this seems to be the hour everyone's either heading home or on to the next place for the evening.

"You know, I have an actual car service we could have used."

She pulls her phone from the pocket of the coat and I silently sigh at the way the lines of the dress are hidden by the merino overcoat. I don't have to be into her to enjoy the sweet curves of her body. "Do you want a gold star?"

But the corner of her mouth lifts as she says that. She's scrolling through different feeds on her phone.

"I live for gold stars," I say.

"Shit." Elliot looks at me. "This is pretty good, but not good enough."

I'm tempted to ask what or make a joke, but I know what she's talking about and it isn't funny.

"We just started, Elliot."

"I know. But we've got four weeks. I've handled last night pretty well, along with what we did tonight, but I think we're going to need extra rules to keep you out of trouble."

"That sounds like a tighter leash."

"It is. Problem is, I don't have any numbers to go on in regards to the board. If I go asking for updates on your progress, then that looks bad. It means you're doing this deliberately."

"I am."

She sighs. "Yes, but the trick is to make it seem like this ultimation or whatever you want to call the letter and your task, is the catalyst for you wanting to change. The world responds to that. The bigger picture here means the smaller one. But with you, I don't have stats to go on."

"So a tighter leash to keep me on the straight and narrow." I tap my fingers against the glass as I watch the traffic and buildings pass slowly on the what should be a quick trip to SoHo. Then I look back at Elliot. "But that makes me look like this is deliberate, too."

"Not if we play it right."

Like her turning up tonight as the woman I'm dating. Is that the life partner shit she was talking about? I'm assuming so, but then again, I don't know what her devious mind has up its devious sleeve.

"And how do we do that?"

"Fill your social calendar. Carefully orchestrate it. Tell me about your family. I've met your mother. But no one else."

We're approaching SoHo, and I lean forward and say to the driver, "Do you have other bookings yet?"

"No, this is my last one."

I reach into my pocket and pull out some crumpled bills. "I've got—" I count the money "—one hundred and fifty to go around the block a few times when we get to the destination."

"You're the boss."

I lean back and look at Elliot. "What did you think of her?"

"You. Charm covering a stubbornness and a manipulative streak. I liked her."

"So you do like me."

"I wouldn't go that far, Ryder..." She flicks to another page on her phone. "But I see where you get certain abilities from. And I think she sees way more and is involved more than you might think."

"You got that from a polite and brief conversation?"

"I'm very good at my job. And I know when someone is fishing for information on me and my family. Which is what she was doing. Checking to see if I was one of your more problematic women."

I pinch the bridge of my nose. "You're a scary-ass female, Perry."

"And you're too good looking for your own good. We all have problems."

I laugh. "I'm the youngest, as you know, and I'm sure you've got this all written down. So let's go with this. We're all getting letters and tasks. Two down and me and Kingston to go. King isn't interested in history or sentimental worth. He likes cold, hard cash. But he's a good guy. We're all good guys, even if I say so myself. We all work fucking hard and while I might play more than them, I work just as hard and meticulously as the rest.

"We have our own businesses and fortunes we built, and we also share some, so we do get together a few times a week for both fun and for work."

"So it's just the rest of the time I need to orchestrate. You can't go out alone anymore, Ryder. Not for the remainder of the four weeks."

Annoyance rises up. "There are times when I have impromptu get togethers with clients. And with friends. A lot of those times were like last night. Business and pleasure."

"Okay." She nods, but I know she's not going to let it go. "I know you're sitting there thinking I don't trust you and you're right. But I also don't trust other women. There are going to be more who pop up for a few minutes worth of fame and you're an idiot if you don't know it. Worse, there's gonna be the ones like the woman you say you don't know."

"I don't."

"Your family—"

"They know I hired someone. I think we covered this—didn't we? Even mother knows, and I'm not putting it past her to have worked out you are that someone."

She sighs again. "This is all good, but you're not hearing me on this. As I was saying, your family is a help and it's even better if they all know someone is helping you improve your life. But it's not enough."

"What are you saying?"

"I'm saying," she says, smiling sweetly, "that your life for the next four weeks is mine."

Something cold trickles through me. "What does that mean, exactly?"

"It means, dear Ryder, you don't breathe or eat or sleep or blink without me knowing."

"What happened to life partner?"

"I tried to get someone, but there wasn't enough time. Welcome to your new girlfriend, your life partner. We're going to be serious as far as the world, aka the board, thinks. We met recently and fell for each other, and more importantly my family means I fit what they see as someone good for Ryder 2.0."

"I meant since when does life partner or serious girlfriend or whatever you want to call it mean jailer?"

"Heard of the old ball and chain?"

"Not funny."

Okay, it is. And the coldness dissipates as her words settle in, along with their meaning. I'm already going to be spending a lot of my time with her during the next four weeks, this just shifts it a little.

I'm okay with it.

I really am. I like her. I like spending time with her. And when you're not plotting your next lust filled move, things are clear and sweet. So yeah, I can do this.

"Fine," I say. I glance at her phone. Something in my chest lurches a little at the photo she's looking at.

It's me and Elliot.

Kissing.

And it does things, seeing that kiss.

I give a thumbs up to the driver to pull over as we once more approach the final destination, her office. My phone buzzes and I pull it out and there's a text.

From Mona. I don't even know who Mona is. But I must have hooked up with her recently and enjoyed it enough to have given her access to the second line on the phone.

I click on the text and oh yeah.

My mouth, your cock. The Taylor.

Now I remember her. That was some blowjob. And the Taylor is her signature move which sounds hokey, but fuck it's hot, and—

"What the actual fuck, Ryder?" Elliot snatches my phone and holds it up at me. "I can't trust you for a second."

Chapter Ten

ELLIOT

I'm so furious, I could commit murder.

Instead, I lean over and shove the door open, giving Ryder barely any time to pay the driver the ridiculous amount he offered him.

On the street, I wave his phone at him. "You're an asshole."

"Give that back." He snatches it from me.

I try to grab it back, but he holds it up high. "This isn't the witch trials, you know. Innocent until proven guilty."

"You were born guilty."

"I didn't do anything. Do you want to see if I texted her first?"

I glare at him. "Yes."

"Too bad. You'll have to trust me." He sucks in a breath and shakes his head and for the first time since I've met him, he's mad. Really mad.

I don't know why. I'm not the one continuously fucking up.

"You have four weeks and—what the hell is the Taylor?"

He doesn't even have the grace to blush. Some woman named Mona—Mona, which has to be some sleazy codename considering the text about his cock and her mouth, just texted an innocent man? I don't think so.

He's a billionaire. He's not going to just hand out his number like he's Joe Biggs from the local pizza joint. So he must have liked the fucking Taylor.

"You don't want to know."

"Maybe I do." Actually, I don't.

"I've half a mind to tell you, but you'd probably combust in a fit of self-righteousness and then I'd have to find someone else to save me."

"Your nobleness and caring knows no bounds."

"I didn't text her. She texted me. And when did I have a chance to text her?"

"Plenty of times this evening."

"The text just came through. You really think women wait?"

I narrow my eyes and think about dumping his ass as a client. But damn, it's a lot of money. And there's a jealous little mean streak in me that likes the idea of him going without for four weeks. It must be agony for the over ego-endowed, beautiful asshat.

"Do you listen to yourself?"

"All the time."

"You are what they call a sleazy asshat. God."

"God is correct." He stops, shoves a hand through his hair and unlocks the phone and thrusts it at me. "There. Check. See? No texts. Just one that came in from someone called Mona."

He's right, and I feel like a horrible person looking, but what am I meant to do? Trust needs to be earned by clients. Especially this one, because my judgment with him is completely in a different country and sambaing to a fantasy of him and me. I make myself breathe slowly and steadily until I'm mostly back under iron control. Or control.

Ryder snatches the phone away and holds it down so I can see as he deletes the text and the number. "Gone. See?"

There's something that looks like hurt in his expression, which is crazy. A man like that doesn't get hurt, not by me, or my accusations that we both know come from the truth of who and what he is. And he likes being that person.

But...he deleted everything from the woman. That must mean something.

A tiny voice inside whispers it's only one incident out of a billion that make up who and what he is. While I can get him to change enough to pull all this off—I hope—I don't know if a man like him can change.

I don't know if a man like him wants to.

And it's not my place.

Only the here and now is.

That's where I have to remain focused.

"Ryder," I say, "you can't delete your past. Your life. It doesn't work that way. I'm...I'm sorry I didn't trust you, but I don't trust clients until they earn it because it's the only way to make things happen. And for you?"

"I'm a lost cause?"

Is he? "No, I mean, our problem is this won't be the last one. It's like I said in the car, these women will keep coming for you, keep tempting you. And over these four weeks that's dangerous. One day, one night, there'll be some babe you want. You'll be tempted and you'll give in."

He pinches the bridge of his nose. "I'm made of stronger stuff than that."

"Or that's why you have me."

Ryder drops his hand and those dark melting chocolate eyes are on me again. He shakes his head a little, like I've hurt him again. But I don't know how. It's all true. And what's more, we both know exactly what he'd rather be doing right now.

"Y'know, Elliot," he says, voice low. It wraps about me, the heat in it belying the cool expression on his face. "Contrary to whatever's in your damn head, I'm not a fucking machine. I don't think about sex every second of the day. I don't have sex the moment I can."

"I didn't—"

"Bullshit." He stalks up to me, closing the small gap and he meets my gaze. "You were thinking that. You were thinking—what's more, your fucking words are saying—I can't control my base urges. I like sex, yes. A lot. I like new experiences. I like to submerge myself in pleasure. But there are times I don't. Times when I'm not interested in the offer, or it's one I know I can't take up. Or you know, life happens. I'm more than a cock."

"Ryder, I'm not saying that." Even though it's in my head. I clench my hands. "But we both know you're easily tempted."

"I have control. When I choose to use it."

We stare at each other. I swallow as a gaggle of people come down the street and I pull Ryder over to the side of the building, near the door. The yellowy light of the streetlamp hits him and he looks for all the world like a fallen angel and it twists hard in my chest.

"You hired me, Ryder. You hired me because you couldn't do this by yourself."

"Yeah, but I didn't think you'd also be judge and jury."

I sigh. "I have to think of every angle. All the time. And you…it's not just reputation, it's who you are. Or," I say, amending slightly, "that reputation is so embedded in you that it comes across as who you are."

His sensuous mouth thins and he nods. "So. What do we do? You're the one with all the damn plans and answers here. You don't trust me. You think I'm barely keeping my dick in my pants—"

"No. I don't think that." I veer away from the trust part. That's way too complicated and I've had too much to drink and I'm punch drunk on the touch of him from that kiss, and from the time spent with him, one on one earlier. "But I need to know you stay away from temptation."

"So you, what? Want me to hand in my phone? So you can check it to make sure I'm not lying or got a piece on the side? That it?"

A horrible idea comes to me. It's the only one I can think of to keep him in line. As one of the few females with power over him as well as one he isn't into, it's the only idea I have in this regard.

"It's worse," I say, digging in my bag for my keys.

His gaze falls to them and then he looks at me. "You have handcuffs?"

"I need you not to engage." I ignore his words. "Not with texts, or emails, or women you meet out. Tell them you're with someone."

"You took care of that."

"One night, that's all, and one night has a way of disappearing if something else pops up. This has to seem real, but up a notch from what we discussed. It's going to be worse than you thought."

"You gonna write me a script? I can handle this."

"You can't." I take hold of his arm, ignoring the heat and zing that slides up through the layers of material to spread out in me. This man is potent. "Is there a cut off time for you?"

"With the four weeks? Or with women?"

I'm tempted to say both. "Your four weeks."

"Four weeks is pretty explanatory, but yeah, things keep shifting, so maybe this needs to be set up for longer, for when all the ink is dried."

We've talked about this, but I need it to really sink in and it has.

At least that part.

"These things have a way of ricocheting. Your scandal, your past, all these women."

"I know."

Does he? I really hope so.

"Worse," Ryder says. "You said worse. How? What way?"

"You're going to spend all your free time with me. Starting tonight. At my place."

"We're already going to be spending our time together." He stops. "Your place?"

There's a beguiling tone in his voice now and I let go of him. "Not like that."

"You're saying spend the night."

"A lot of nights, Ryder."

He smooths his fingers through my hair and I shiver, my body melting inside out. "I think I'd like that."

For a moment, a vision comes to me, of him looking at me the way I know he looks at women. Of that mouth, those kisses being mine, of exploring his body, him wanting me. And I want to kick myself for such stupid fantasies. He doesn't want me. Not like that.

I sigh. "Come on Romeo, we're going to my place."

"So forward."

He's in his comfort zone, and the light flirt I can deal with. Light flirt is a simple conversation to him.

"No time like the present to do this."

I step forward and punch in the key code, then unlock the door.

"You live in your office?"

"The top floor is mine." I don't look at him as I go in and head for the elevator. "Come on."

I come out of the bathroom, in my pajamas—he's already seen me in them and who the hell am I going to impress if I whip out lingerie I don't have and pretend I sleep in make-up? Let's face it, this is Ryder Sinclair who has his pick of the world's most beautiful women—and he's poking about the living room.

"You have plants."

"I know," I say.

His jacket and coat are off, his vest that fits slim against him is still on and damn, in the narrow dress pants and vest that are such a deep chocolate they could be black cut, he is a breathtaking figure of manhood.

I take another moment to admire the deep, dark wine of the shirt, which is rolled up at the sleeves to the elbows. The color shouldn't work, but it does. It somehow manages to be him and subdued, but now, unfettered by the jacket, it's all him, understated flamboyance. That fashionista edge.

The intricate line work of his tattoo disappears up under his sleeve and from here I can see a dancing skeleton with touches of color here and there along the winding vine of thorn and flowers and leaves.

What am I doing?

Good question, and whatever it is, I need to stop. I drag in a breath and raise my eyes. He's studying the velvet lines of the philodendron gloriosum. The large heart-shaped leaves have striking white veins on it. And they're not complete divas or drama queens like some plants I've had.

Then Ryder turns to me, a soft smile turning his mouth up as he runs his gaze over me. "And there she is."

"I've been here the entire night."

"Not that quirky heart of you. That was hidden beneath the hot dress and face."

"Are you saying I'm Eleanor Rigby?"

"Maybe you are." He hums a few bars of the old Beatles song. "You also like to hide. But there's no hiding when old school Godzilla comes out to play."

My hand clenches. "I wasn't expecting company."

"And I'm not complaining."

"You're just...what?"

He shrugs and the air crackles and sings. "Figuring you out."

"Nothing to figure out." I stomp off and grab some bedding from the closet in my tiny study. There really isn't a hall, it's more rooms leading from the central nerve system of the living room. I dump the pillow, quilt, and sheets on the floor next to the burnt sienna velvet art deco sofa with its curved back and plush cushions.

"I beg to differ."

"You would."

His smile burns brighter and makes me hot inside. "I'm just saying you're complex, a puzzle, and I'm putting together the pieces."

Ryder starts to make up the sofa without me. I'm so shocked I watch him.

He raises a brow as he finishes tucking in a corner of the sheet. "What? You think I have a man servant who does everything including brush my teeth?"

"No. You'd have a woman."

"Hey, I take offense at that." He throws the pillow into place and unbuttons the vest and I find it suddenly hard to swallow. "I'd have more…interesting roles for her to play."

"You're incorrigible."

"Guilty."

I need to get out of here. Go to my room and pretend to sleep. And not think he's out here. The upside of Ryder-induced insomnia is time to work.

"The kitchen is through there—" I point to the left and then the right "and the bathroom's there."

"You know, it's not too late."

My heart starts to thump wildly. "Too late for what?"

"Getting the fuck out of here and going to my place. You can babysit me just as easily there."

"I'm not babysitting you."

"Whatever you want to call it. I'm just saying my place is bigger."

"And I don't care. Goodnight, Ryder."

I hurry to my room and try to sleep. When that doesn't work, I try some work. But it's hard to concentrate, knowing Ryder Sinclair is outside my door. On my sofa.

In the end, I turn the TV on that I rarely use that's in my room, mounted to the wall. I turn the sound on low. There's a Golden Girls rerun on and I let Rose, Blanche, Dorothy and Sophia's antics wash over me, the darkness only broken by the images on the screen.

I'm almost asleep when the bed shifts and someone slides in next to me.

Ryder.

"What the hell," I say as I turn, suddenly wide awake, "do you think you're doing?"

Chapter Eleven

Ryder

"Sleeping here."

She's glaring at me and suddenly this great idea doesn't seem that great. In the light of the Golden Girls, it seems a little iffy.

"Your sofa's too small. It's pretty and I'm sure it's comfortable to sit on, but not to sleep. I'm six two. I'm not made for sofa sleeping. And this bed is big."

"If you say just right, Goldilocks," she says, grumpiness infusing her words and sending a bright spark of warmth through my blood, "I'll bite you."

"Do your fangs come out after midnight? I haven't fed you."

"That's Gremlins, not vampires, idiot. Go back to the sofa. This is not for you."

I know that. I'm not an idiot. She might sometimes look at me like I'm a delicious dessert she wants to devour, but she doesn't actually want me. And I don't want her, no matter how fascinating she is. No matter how good she tasted.

Elliot would probably cause bodily harm if I made a move, and I sort of find that refreshing. She's like no one or nothing I've known. And falling asleep with her has the markings of a different kind of pleasure.

"I know that," I say, trying to reassure her of my noble intentions, "as *if* I'd make a move on you."

Elliot kicks me and makes a snorting sound. "I know that. I get it."

There's something about the way she says it that rouses curiosity. "Why do you say that?"

"You said that."

"I meant..." I sigh. "I meant I'm not going to maul you or seduce you. That's not my style."

"Yes, it is. The latter, anyway. I haven't heard anything about unwanted maulings."

"I meant the... you get it."

"I'm not the kind of woman you want. We know that. Do you have to keep on about it?"

No one's been going on about it. At least not in the way she means. "I just thought it might be nicer to be in a big bed."

"Be my guest."

The sarcasm is clear and I ignore it, sliding in closer to her, the scent of gardenias is a lingering, subtle gift to the air if I breathe close enough to her. It makes me want to move in closer, but I don't.

"Thanks."

Deep down, I didn't come in here just because the thought of her bed over the sofa is more enticing. It is. It's a bed. It contains space and a warm body and one I know I can fall asleep next to.

But I didn't stand, dithering for the first time in my life, outside her door like a teenager for that. Even if I'd wanted to just go to sleep in the same bed as a woman, I'd go in. I can pick up when and if I'm wanted, and I knew she wouldn't kick me out.

Actually...

No. I didn't know that.

I knew she'd get it. That it wasn't a big seduction event, or me simply taking what I want, when I want.

I simply didn't know if she'd tell me to go. And I'd have gone. Of course I would have. Climbing in bed with her was already a line crossed. I'm just not sure what that line is.

But I know why I did it.

I like being around her. And there was a loneliness I couldn't shake out in the living room, something I didn't know existed. Being here, with her, it's gone. This feels right.

Because she's Elliot.

A friend, I think. A female friend.

It's a new experience so I'm still finding my way, and there's so much about her that's unexpectedly delicious, like the way I can tease and she flares up beautifully.

She shifts beneath the covers and her soft cotton-covered leg brushes mine.

"That," she says, "was sarcasm."

"I know." I pick up a lock of her hair from her haphazard ponytail, fighting the urge to release the soft and silky mass. In the light of the TV, there are strands of gold and caramel amongst the red. "But you're not going to kick me out."

"I should."

"You won't."

"No, I won't. As long as you behave, which we both know you will."

"Because," I say, "I'm a gentleman."

"Do not make me laugh."

But I smile as I ease her into my arms, just so we're more comfortable. For a moment she goes stiff then she makes a small sound that does very untoward things to my libido and she softens, melting into me.

She feels good. I almost tell her she made that weird, empty loneliness go away, but once said I can't take the words back. Elliot might laugh. I know others would. Big, bad Ryder Sinclair getting in bed with a woman to chase the ghost of loneliness away. Yeah, they would all laugh.

Not at who I'm with, not at all. With her smoky voice and intriguing mouth and Rita Hayworth hair, not to mention that sharp wit and brain, I'm shocked men aren't fighting to be where I am. No, they'd laugh because of how pathetic I'd sound.

"So the Golden Girls, huh?"

"Are we talking now?"

"Unless you can think of something else."

"Sleep," she says, "I can think of that."

"It's so overrated. I'd have pictured you the Gilda type."

"I'm not pigeonhole material, Ryder."

She knows the old film I'm talking about, it's in her voice and somehow, it heartens me.

"I didn't say you were. But you've got this edge of another time." Her furniture in the living room, even the frame of the bed and the pieces in the bedroom, they're all art deco, and they're real. I'd bet money on it.

All lovingly restored. All respected. It's like her plants. I don't know what they are, not the ones in here, but they're beautiful pieces of living art, tactile and...things she cares for, things she makes the center of attention, not herself.

It's another piece to the Elliot Perry puzzle.

Her fingers slip against my arm a moment before she pulls her hand away, but I take it and rest it on my bare chest, where she curls her fingers into a ball. She sighs. "Do you always get your way and are you calling me old fashioned?"

"Sometimes, and maybe, but not the way you think. You're something different, and I like it. I can talk to you."

"Well, at least I'm good for something."

I ignore the ice in her voice and pull her further against me, so I'm comfortable and from her little sigh, she is, too. I toy with her hair. "You are." The old ladies talk on the TV, and canned laughter follows and I close my eyes, breathing her in, letting the warmth and softness of her meld into me. "Why did you choose to live above your damn office?"

Startled, she shifts, and almost hits a very important part of me, one I'm very fond of. "I love this building. I actually had this converted to an apartment. Or back to an apartment. It was empty office space when I got it."

"Just get an apartment."

"Of course you'd say that. Out with the old, up with the new, that it?"

I smile against her hair, and rest my other arm over her middle, buried in the soft white quilt. "You have to step up your insult game, Perry. You know that's not how I operate, unless, of course, you didn't do your homework."

"How dare you." But she doesn't sound that mad. She shifts again and goes still and that something—my cock—she almost hit, this time she does, but just a soft brushing against it and that sweet, electric buzz of arousal shoots through me even harder. The arousal I've so far been ignoring. "You have an erection."

She says this like it's an insult.

"I'm aware. Don't worry, I won't molest you."

Elliot sniffs like some outraged Victorian spinster. "I know. You don't want me."

All the evidence right now points way in the other direction, but I like her and I'm not about to fuck up this friendship by a quick grope when nothing's gonna come from it.

"Look," I say. "You're female, you're soft and you fit. I want. That's how I'm built. But I like you, Elliot. A lot. So I'm not going to do anything about it. Okay? Rest easy. You can save your smelling salts for another time."

"Where on Earth did you learn all your references? You're so weird."

I laugh at her slightly mollified, slightly annoyed tone. "Would you believe I was a lonely child?"

She doesn't answer for a long moment. "Yeah, I'd believe that. Like you don't fit."

"Boarding school will do that to you. And, well, you get it, growing up rich."

"We have money," she corrects, "but we're old name more than Sinclair rich. You're in a different stratosphere."

"Our father was a slave driver. It instilled us with a great work ethic but little else, and I was the dreamer."

"That why you got the tattoo?"

"I forget about it, which is weird. I think because I wasn't even twenty when I got it, or started it. The thing's part of me."

She traces a finger along one of the dancing skeletons. "It reminds me of the three."

My heart beats a little faster. "The three?"

"Dante's Divine Comedy."

"Really?"

"It's silly, but—"

"It's not silly, because it is. I was obsessed with it when I was a kid."

The tattoo stretches up over my shoulder to take over my back in a watercolor tattoo, but I don't want to talk about me. I'd rather talk about her.

"Really?"

"Do you have to keep sounding so damn surprised, Perry. You do a man's ego harm."

She snorts. "I don't think a nuke could harm your ego, Sinclair."

"Do you think it would give me super powers?"

"Don't!" She groans and goes to move away, but I'm not ready to let her go yet. She feels too good. "I don't think womankind is ready for that."

I just laugh. Who knew talking and lazy flirting with no agenda other than just being could be so much fun? In a bed? When I'm only wearing my underwear and a hard on that's going to have to just deal with itself.

Either that or a trip to the bathroom—

No. No way am I doing that and risking getting caught. I'd never live it down with someone like Elliot Perry.

"Fine. But I'm not that bad."

"You're worse. And if you keep going, I might end up liking you."

I pause. "Is that a bad thing?"

"Yes. No. I don't know." There's something heavy in the air, but whatever it is she doesn't say it. "I was planning on simply admiring your face and hating you."

I want to ask what she was going to say, but I don't want to break the mood. "I am pretty handsome."

"Oh, yep, there we are. Back to hate."

"You don't."

"I do."

"I think your plants like me. Did you see that velvety one perk up when I touched her leaves?"

She pinches my chest and pulls away. This time I let her, but she rolls over on her side to look at me, tucking her hands beneath her cheek. "My philodendron? Plants aren't known for their leafy intelligence, Ryder."

"I'll tell them—"

"Don't you dare."

Her eyes sparkle, and like this she's almost heartbreakingly pretty in that Elliot way. It's something in her that shifts, like I can see a sliver of her soul and it's breathtaking.

"Well, you did agree to share your bed with me, so maybe I won't."

"I didn't agree to anything. You climbed in, unasked."

I rise up a little on one elbow, pulling the pillow on my side down to my chest. I'm cold. "You didn't kick me out. No court would convict me."

"You're a very strange, sad man."

"I'll take pity. Hey, should I develop a limp?"

"Idiot."

"So," I say, "you're the middle child, aren't you?"

"How do you figure?"

I didn't mean for that to come out, but thinking about it, that fits. "I'm the youngest. Spoiled, and I got away with things King and the others didn't. That happens with the youngest. I know you come from a biggish family, too. And the Perry kids all did things to put themselves out there. Except you."

She looks down, bright spots of color blooming on her throat and cheek. "I'm not the out there type. People don't notice me."

"I do."

Her gaze slams into mine. "Only because you hired me. Come on. If I walked into a room you'd barely notice me."

I want to say that's not true. And now I've gotten a glimpse of her beneath it all, I would most definitely notice her, but she's right. If I didn't know her I wouldn't. And I'd be missing out.

What the fuck does that say about me?

"Then I'm a complete moron," I say. "You—"

"I'm tired. We should go to sleep."

She's got a point. Although I could talk and tease and flirt with her until the sun came up. There are other things I could do, too. But I don't say any of that because I like living.

She switches off the television. It doesn't take long for her to fall asleep, and I watch her as a sliver of light comes in through her arched window.

Like this, she's soft and sweet, and innocent. And I think she might be innocent—by my standards. She's fresh and lovely and I inch a little closer to her until we're almost touching.

The heat of her warms me and a calmness comes down over me.

I close my eyes as the sound of New York wafts up from the streets below, and let sleep start to take me away.

And as I drift off, it comes to me that this might be the first time I've slept with a woman.

As in *slept* slept with a woman.

She's both a difficult and easy person, and the longer I spend with her, the more I like her and I know I don't want to give this up, this seeing her, knowing her, when the four weeks are up.

And this? Right here? Right now?

I like it.

What the hell am I becoming?

Chapter Twelve

ELLIOT

There's a heavy warmth in me, on me. And it feels good. Like all is right in the world.

I suddenly go still.

I'm not alone.

Everything last night comes tumbling back.

Ryder Sinclair is in my bed, and that warm heaviness is him. An arm is around me and one leg over mine.

I believe the words here are *oh, shit*.

Slowly, I edge out from beneath him, freezing when his arm tightens a moment. He mutters something, and a small frown appears and I can't help it...I take a second to appreciate the sheer beauty of him sleeping. He's softer in sleep, more accessible. Which is nothing more than a fallacy and very dangerous.

With his arm on me, the winding tattoo is up close and the skeletons are delicate and intricate with the flowers and thorns and vines coming from their hands. I want to touch them, but sanity prevails and I drag my mind from fantasyland and back to the Great Escape.

Ryder shifts and turns over, somehow stealing all the covers with him.

I slide off the bed completely and start to rise when a hand clamps around my wrist, holding me there, setting me ablaze with that connection.

"You're no fun, Elliot."

His voice first thing is surprisingly awake, low, and warm. There's humor there, and it all takes its toll. It's a nice toll, sweet, and something I don't want. I try and tug free.

He doesn't let go.

I bite back a sigh. "I'm a lot of fun. I just need to get a start on the day."

"Your project is already here." He's not holding me there anymore. His hand is still on me, though, his fingers a slow slide against my flesh and that caress is more binding than any cold steel snapped onto my wrist could ever be. "And pajama parties have rules. Like…no sneaking off."

I pretend I'm made of stronger stuff and keep my tone crisp and edged with sarcasm. "Have you ever been to a pajama party?"

"I went to boarding school. Does torture count?"

"That's a no, then?"

"And she's cruel…" The smile in his tone warms me. "No. But this is my pajama party, and my rules. Come on. We don't have to get up yet."

I sigh and sit on the bed. "Not getting up somehow morphs into rules?"

"I'm gifted that way?" He lets me go and throws back the covers, patting the empty spot.

Just call me a giant idiot weakling, but the flash of near naked, sleep-warmed man crumbles resolve, and I slide back in.

"This is ridiculous. We have a day to get through, and—"

"Everyone needs a little ridiculousness in their lives." Ryder's hand comes to rest on my thigh. "Like take what's going on with me. It's all insane on a level I don't want to think about. Why should it matter what I do outside of doing the job?"

"Because, Ryder," I say, "as much as you want to go forth and practice spreading your seed—"

"Ouch."

"—you can't if you want all the things you want. Money sometimes doesn't talk as loudly as reputation."

"I'm not a whore."

I give him a look and he raises his brows even as a small, sheepish smile plays.

"Okay," he says, "you and your puritanical ways might think I am, but I'm not."

"If we're talking traditional sense, then no."

"I like having a good time. Don't you?"

"There's more to life than that."

I sound like the worst fun-murderer out there. Give me fun and I'll kill it for you. He's probably thinking that, actually.

"There's boredom, but I'm not into that. I like women. I like sensuality. I like feeling good. And as I said, I do my job and as ridiculous as all this is, I'm doing it. Obeying the law of the land, dead-father-style."

I study him a moment. "You don't care about him?"

"I loved my father," he says quietly. "But he was a hard man to love. An easy man to respect, but love? He didn't hand it out string-free. It's been a year since he passed, but in a way he's been gone for much longer than that. To us, anyway. I guess he was the push the bird out of the nest and move on type. Or, so it seemed."

He turns to face me and for a moment I can't think of anything to say. It all sounds sad and I wonder what the little boy he was felt. "I'm sorry."

"Don't be. And it's too early for this."

"You started it."

"You didn't want to talk about you and your aversion to fun." He stops, his gaze skimming over me, and I fight the urge to pull the covers up as my nipples bead under that look.

"You didn't hire me to be fun."

He completely ignores me. "I'm amending that. You act like you have an aversion to it, but you're a lot of fun, once you get going."

"Wow," I say, with heaping amounts of dry sarcasm. "Thanks. You're a real flatterer."

"I didn't mean that."

"You didn't mean to flatter me? Good thing because you didn't. I think the word's insult."

Ryder laughs, propping himself a little higher with his elbow on a pillow, and he draws a pattern on my thigh, over the quilt. "I didn't mean you're anything like a bore. I meant you're interesting and a good time when you don't try and...disappear."

"I do nothing of the kind." This is true. I can't help it if I somehow fade into the background. "Besides, it's my job to not be seen."

Ryder sighs. "I had a good time because of you."

My head starts a slow spin. His fingers are magic and his words...

"I know you're not hitting on me." I make myself pull away from him and get to slightly unsteady feet.

"Of course not." He rolls on his back and tucks the pillow under his head. "I wouldn't do that."

I stare at him, shaking my head as I try and think of something to say. Instead, I turn away and start grabbing things to take to the bathroom with me so I can emerge dressed and ready for the day. "I know you wouldn't."

"Elliot—"

"Stop. You have to get to work. I have to get to work for you. We have our plan to push forward."

And I don't wait for his answer. Instead, like the coward with a healthy dose of self-preservation that I am, I hurry into the bathroom like there's a demon in my bed, instead of a man.

Demon, I think, locking the door, might not be too far off.

My day passes in a flurry of micromanagement and casting longer threads out.

Ryder's at work, where he's assured me in twenty texts that he's behaving. And by that he means Elliot style, not Ryder style.

His words. Not mine.

There's an event tonight. Boring and staid in his words, mine too, not that I'd admit it to him.

Nothing like a stodgy fundraiser that's more about a tick on the resume and being seen by the right sort of old money and old-school Fortune 500 company execs than the charity in question.

I'm going with him because after last night, it's the smart thing to do. Perhaps not smart personally for me, but smart for him, and he's paying me a lot of money, so I can just swallow down the misgivings with a lot of dollar signs.

I finish my day, shoot Ryder a text with the door code to the building, and after people have gone, I stay in my office tying up little loose ends and generally controlling everything.

Getting ready isn't going to take me long, I know that, but I still find myself, when I take the elevator to my apartment, spending longer than I ever would.

For what, is what I'd like to know. So Ryder, a man I both want and don't want and know will never look at me in that way I crave, will fail to be impressed?

He's seen me in my pajamas. He's seen me first thing in the morning. He's told me I'm the last person he'd flirt with...

"Idiot."

Still...

I'm checking my hair for the millionth time when my door buzzes.

Ryder looks spectacular in one of the suits. "Money speaks," he says as I give him a long twice-over. "But even so, I suspect you had something to do with the speed of suit one's arrival by courier today."

It's black and the cut classic with a modern edge. "You think I greased the wheel?"

"No." He laughs. "I think you can make things happen that could be classed as miracles."

I hate myself, but heat rushes through me, bright and warming at his words.

"You're on time." I grab my purse, and sweeping him out the door reluctantly take the arm he offers.

The fewer times I touch him, the better.

We arrive at the fundraiser for underprivileged private school children—I should be blasé about some of the genteel mega rich fundraisers, but I'm not because I can think of so many other things that deserve their money apart from an exclusive school—and it's as boring and staid as Ryder moaned about the entire trip here.

He comes up to me, his fingers light and low on my back, sending tendrils of electricity tumbling through me. "This is to do...what?"

"Keep the riff-raff out of your schools while looking like you let them in."

He laughs and takes a sip of champagne, my champagne that he purloins with a smooth move. "You're not exactly poor or from the riff-raff, Perry."

"Compared to you, I'm the offspring of chimney sweeps."

"I can think of worse jobs."

"Idiot."

"You like me." Then he groans. "Here comes trouble."

His mother approaches, all smiles and discreet, tasteful jewels and a tailored suit. Her gaze flickers to Ryder. "Off with you. But not too far."

"Mother—"

"Now." Her expression isn't one to allow argument, even though Ryder clearly wants to do just that.

He thinks better of it and slinks off with my champagne.

"Don't think I'm fooled," Faye Sinclair says. "About the girlfriend thing."

Of course she isn't.

"You're way too good for him, much as I love him. Ryder's a...work in progress, and worth it, if he can get over himself."

I stare at her. We spoke the night before, and he told me his family knows he hired someone.

"Well—"

"I like you, Elliot. I think you're what he needs."

Of course she likes me. Mothers always do. "I'm not sure what you mean."

"The letter, the job. It's not a secret."

This should flood me with relief, hearing it not just from Ryder, but from his mother, but for some reason, it doesn't. I give her a speculative look. She only smiles.

"You could give him a pass," I say.

"This thing, it's more complicated than Ryder thinks." She turns her champagne glass. "It's not just about the outer image."

"It's about change. But in what way? Ryder's Ryder. How he is outside of work doesn't affect his job."

"As I said, it's complicated."

"And you're in charge of this."

She pauses to say hello to a passing senator. Then she refocuses on me. "I'm overseeing things."

It's clear to me she's pulling whatever strings she feels like pulling, but there isn't a hint of malice about her. Whatever she's up to is for Ryder's sake. And it isn't my job to judge. It's my job to make sure Ryder gets what he wants.

"Inner change can come, but in four weeks?"

Faye sets a firm, warm hand on my upper arm and squeezes gently. "As you said, Ryder's Ryder. He is capable of change."

"If he wants that."

"Yes." There's a small smile right before she takes a sip of her drink. "If."

"You're aware of my job here, so if you have anything I need—"

"There's a lot at stake, Elliot."

"Okay, but if I'm helping him, how does that do anything? You know with the four weeks change will be mostly cosmetic." I'm saying this, not because I want to, but because it feels the right thing to say. His mother isn't the kind of woman to take to bullshit. I want—need—to see what her game is.

"I'm the one judging, as I know him best."

I nod. "So you're willing to just say he's changed?"

"If he changes, yes."

I really wish Ryder hadn't taken my drink. I could do with something to occupy my hands. Instead, I keep them by my side. Image goes a long way with others. "Why would you do that, say he's changed if he ticks all the boxes, when you know he hired me?"

"I'm his mother."

"Not some all-seeing being." I decide to push it. "I said inner change can come, but after a long, hard slog; after effort and micro shifts. People don't change. Not in four weeks."

"Elliot," she says, "that's where you're wrong. People can and they do. And there's a lot more to my youngest son than there might seem."

"I'm keeping my judgments to myself."

His mother laughs. "You're too good for him, but he's got it in him to rise to that level."

I stare at her. "Ryder and I...there's nothing there. He's not interested and I'm not what he wants."

"I'm just saying," she says, "that if anyone's up to the job of implementing a life change in Ryder, it would be you. The trick is, Ryder can't do just a cover up that lasts up to the end of the four weeks. It has to be that something in him really changes."

"I don't think he sees it that way."

"Not yet."

"Does he know about this?" I ask.

Faye only smiles and it's clear Ryder doesn't know. Not on a deep down level, not...whatever it is she's hinting at.

"Elliot," she says, "the trick here he doesn't and he shouldn't. You need to bring this fundamental change in him. One he doesn't see coming, and you can't discuss this with him. Do the job as you both planned, but I like you, so I wanted you to know I'm looking for something else—"

"Like what?"

"I'll know it when I see it."

What the hell have I gotten myself into here? "You want me to bring about some kind of magical change in him that I don't know what it is, and neither does he?"

"Exactly."

"Oh, well, in that case," I say, letting the sarcasm out, "that sounds easy." I stop, look at her. "Are you going to offer me more money for this?"

Faye takes another sip of champagne. "Would you take it?"

"No." There's not even a question. "I just want to know what it is you're actually asking."

"What the fuck are you two talking about?"

We both turn and there's Ryder. Waiting.

Chapter Thirteen

RYDER

"Now, Ryder, language," my mother says with the kind of breeze people use to hide all kinds of things behind.

"I asked a question."

I shift my gaze from my mother to Elliot, whose red hair is cascading from the glittering comb holding it up. This isn't a deliberate effect; her hair's escaping and it gives her a soft freshness I appreciate. I also appreciate the dark burnt orangey-black velvet dress that has a very thirties style about it. But that and her luscious, fascinating mouth aside, I'm not appreciating the lack of answers.

From either of them.

My mother isn't about to talk, not unless she wants to, and I'm beginning to think there's an ulterior motive why they were discussing money.

"Elliot?"

She has an air of caught red-handed, but that fades and steel and composure move in and damned if the two of them haven't been infused with the same sort of sneaky stubbornness I don't like. Mainly because I get my stubborn streak from the well preserved woman calling herself my mother.

"I heard something about money." I take a swallow of the new glass of champagne I grabbed. "And a suspicious man might think that's to do with him. I'm a very suspicious man."

"I tried to steal her away to work for me, but she wasn't having it." My mother air kisses me and slides a glance at Elliot and then she's gone, disappearing into the boring and too-moneyed—an irony not lost on me—crowd.

"Well?"

Elliot just sighs and takes the champagne from me. She doesn't drink it, simply holds it, like she needed a lifeline or something similar. "It was nothing."

"Really?" I lean in and say against her ear, "sure looked like something."

"Don't crowd me." She gives me a little shove with the glass flute of golden liquid. "She knows you hired me."

"Of course she does." I take a tiny step back. "She's not an idiot."

"If she didn't buy me as your girlfriend, then I don't know about everyone else."

I grin. "She's a smart woman. She gets it from me."

"That's not how things work, Ryder."

"Of course she knows we wouldn't be dating." Because she is a smart woman. My mother knows a woman like Elliot would turn me down flat. I only know this because Elliot's the only woman like Elliot I know, and something tells me that's exactly what would happen. If I was interested, of course. "And—"

"You don't need to rub it in." Elliot starts to stalk away, but I grab her arm and pull her back to me.

She looks up at me.

I want to say a whole lot of shit to her, but it all is so absurd I don't. Elliot always misconstrues me, anyway. She thinks she's got me pigeonholed. She's probably got some kind of thesis, too.

"Rub what in? And why are you so huffy?"

Her eyes narrow. "I'm not huffy."

"Yeah, you are. You have little sparks about you. Not actual ones, but I can feel them."

"Look—"

"No, you listen." If I let her speak, if I let her go, she'll stomp out and our time's limited. I don't know what my mother said to get Elliot so riled, but it doesn't matter. I need to smooth things, and I do that well. Usually. With people who aren't named Elliot Perry. "My mother might have worked it out, but no one else would."

"No one would believe it."

"People believe all sorts of things."

"No, that you'd want someone as unflashy as me."

"I don't just go for flashy, Perry. I'm not crass."

Her face says otherwise, so I ignore it.

"I'm a man of many talents," I add. "Of many tastes and types. People believe whatever you give them if it's sold well enough."

She shakes her head and suddenly I don't want this conversation to happen here. I want the night off. I want to capture a little of that laid back fun from the night before.

"Maybe you're right," she says.

"Of course I am. Let's get out of here, Perry."

For a moment I think she's going to say no, but wheels turn in that head of hers. I can almost hear them. Then she smiles, and it's the sort of smile that could undo a man. "Okay. Dancing."

"Excuse me?"

"You heard me. Let's sell this. Let's go dancing."

I'm staring at her. Of all the things I figured she'd come up with...dancing—of any kind—is the last.

"What?" There's an innocent air I don't trust.

I point a finger at her. "Like a club? Or salsa? Are you a secret waltzer?"

"You're an idiot, no. Just out, music, dancing, you know."

"Enlighten me."

"You're changing, Ryder. Let's show change."

"By boogying?"

"Do people boogy still?"

"I don't know. This is your lame idea."

"It's not lame, Sinclair." She tilts her head to the side. "Unless, of course, you're afraid of dancing."

"Me? Never. Let's go."

I want to say the place is jumping, but while it might not be doing that, it's got life, and it's totally down to the ground in all the unexpected ways that should be expected.

The place is so low-key I didn't even catch the name. There was a sign on the door, but as she led me here, right into the heart of the Village where on the street we're completely overdressed, but in here, not at all, I just followed along.

We're led to a table in the back by a sexily but tastefully clad waitress, reminiscent of the old world cigarette girls. There in the back under golden lights, a band plays and people dance.

Yep, there's actual dancing.

Others sit around and chat and laugh and drink. And it's got a low-key yet glam vibe I like.

Never in a million years would I think such a place exists, or if I did, of coming here.

It's a date, not sex.

I take that back as we place an order for drinks, and Elliot pulls the combs from her hair and shakes it free.

This place is date and sex with someone special. This is long, sensuous sex. This is smolder. This can be none of the above. This can be fun or serious conversation. It's a blank canvas with the paints set out.

I lean forward and take the combs from her as Elliot goes to put her hair back up. Call me an old-fashioned asshole, but I like her hair free.

"Give me those."

"No. It looks good like that."

She snatches them from me but doesn't twist her hair up and shove them in place. "Is this free advice from the Ryder Sinclair fashion hour?"

"Yes."

Elliot laughs and tucks the combs in her purse as the waitress returns with the side cars—I followed her lead this evening.

The music flows around us and I smooth a wayward strand of hair from her face, trying not to notice how soft and smooth and warm her skin is beneath my fingers. "I feel like I'm in one of those movies from the Fifties. If Dean Martin comes out to sing with the big band, I'm not going to be surprised."

"I will be, considering he's been dead for a long time."

"You know what I mean," I say, smiling.

"Yeah." Elliot toys with her glass. "I don't get to come here often, but this part of the Village, where tiny gems of arts and music and theater exist for themselves, is special. And I love it."

I sip my drink. "You're an interesting one, Perry."

"I'm really not."

"You really are. This...this is perfect."

Her cheeks blush and I want to slide the coolness of my glass over them. Maybe let some of the condensation drip down, fall on her decolletage and—I stop the down and dirty direction of my thoughts.

"Or," I say, "didn't you expect me to appreciate a place like this?"

Her mouth twists in a tiny smile. "To be fair, you're not exactly Mr. Deep and Meaningful to the world."

The words poke at me, and I'm not sure why. She's got a point. "I'm more man whore, huh?"

"I didn't..." She sucks in a breath. "I don't take people here much, Ryder. You like beautiful things and this... I think this is beautiful."

"It's a nod to the past but modern," I say, looking about and clapping as the band finishes a song. "It's also not kitsch. At least, not in the cringe-kitsch way so many places have. I really like it."

"I believe this actually used to be one of those supper clubs," she says. "The owner bought it years ago and revamped it from a beer soaked dive to this. I guess tonight is big band, but sometimes it's salsa, or jazz or whatever pops up. Anyway, I'm glad you like it."

I try and ignore the tone that holds surprise. She doesn't think I'd like a place like this, but she's wrong. I want to say one reason I like it is because it seems so utterly her. And it's got depth. But that all sounds so...I don't know...pathetic, that I keep it to myself. Instead, as the band starts a slow number, I get up and hold out my hand.

"You want to dance?"

"Of course I do. You were the one who suggested it and taunted."

She doesn't move and I frown.

"What's the matter?"

Elliot looks at me, the people slow dancing behind me, then picks up her glass and drains it and I'm honestly not sure whether to be insulted or laugh. "Dutch courage?"

"Something like that."

She places her hand in mine and it's cool, a small zing to the senses. Just the reaction to the temperature change from the glass, I tell myself, but as I close my fingers around hers, I wonder.

Because she's a bundle of sparks and barbs and depths and mountains. She's secrets and wide fields. Storms and sunny skies.

The song is slow and smoky and winds around us as I settle her in against me. And we sway to the music.

Elliot's warm and soft and the curves perfect to hold. And the gardenias are there, twined with that something belonging to her alone. A something which slides in low against the senses. It's something I can get behind.

"Loosen up, Perry."

"Not every woman falls at your feet," she snaps.

I laugh. "I'm aware. God forbid if they did. But I'm not that repulsive that you can't put your arms around me."

Those sweet eyes meet mine. "And if I don't want to?"

"Pretend, that's what the evening's about, remember."

Elliot makes a small sound of huffy suffering and I laugh against her ear as she slides her arms up and around my neck.

It's not much of a dance, but it's the kind that any man worth his salt loves. A woman to hold, her body against his. The possibilities are endless. And I know I have to stop thinking like that. First off, it's Elliot. She'd probably punch me if she thought my mind kept going there with her. Second...I need to prove to myself I can actually do this. Just be with a woman like her, one with so many possibilities, and not twist it into anything. I need to just be.

Because if I'm like this around her, thinking of that mouth, the taste of her, and what else would be good with her, then I'm a hopeless case.

I don't want to change.

I shouldn't have to change.

But if I can't, even for a while, then I'm just as pathetic as she seems to think I am.

Jesus. Did they put self-pity juice in the side car?

"Happy?"

"Yeah," I say, easing her a little closer. "I am."

And apart from that self-pity juice, it's true. She feels right. If she feels right, then...

"You know, Perry, I think this is going to work."

Something in her gaze darkens. "The scam?"

"It's not a scam. Not really. It's me fitting into what I have to for four weeks. With you with me? Easy?"

"Sinclair," she says, her fingers a flirt against the skin of my nape, tangling with some of my hair as we dance, "life and things aren't that easy. Even for you."

"C'mon, I got you, babe."

She rolls her eyes. "Look what happened to Sonny and Cher."

"You're like a walnut."

"If that's your flirting game, then it's a good thing you're a pretty man, otherwise..." And Elliot steps on my toes. Deliberately. I know this because of the satisfied curl to her mouth. "You have problems."

"I meant, hard on the outside and it takes effort to crack you, but I'm thinking once someone does, then it's sweet and luscious right there, on the inside. Delicious."

She shivers and breathes in deep. "Stop that."

"Stop what?"

"You know what."

This time I smile. "Make me. I also think we look good together."

She looks at me with suspicion. "You and me? I don't think so."

I want to taste her lips again, I realize. I want to close that gap and kiss her. And I don't have an excuse for it. At all. I just want it.

"I don't think we should do this." She starts to pull away, but I tighten my hold.

"We need to. What if people are watching?"

"That's an occupational hazard for you, being you. Rich or poor, people are definitely going to be watching you."

Elliot pulls away again and this time, I let her, catching her hand as she does so and twining our fingers as we head back to our table.

I get another round of drinks, watching Elliot like she's the most fascinating thing in the room. And that's probably because to me, right now, she is.

"Why the hell do you think it's what people do to me?"

"Watch you?" Our drinks arrive and she picks hers up. "That's what they do. That waitress couldn't take her eyes off you. You're a beautiful man."

"You say that like it's a crime."

She frowns. "I'm just stating that's what happens, Ryder."

"People look at you, too."

I don't do this. I don't push and scratch at surfaces, I don't dissect the pretty girl I'm with. I don't do any of what I'm doing with Elliot to anyone else.

But maybe that's because I don't usually like them, not in that way. The ones I'm friends with I've known forever. Or they're family. And women hand me whatever I want.

Except for Elliot.

Maybe it's the challenge, but I don't think so. It's something more, deeper. I like her.

And I've never had a female friend.

I take a deep swallow of my drink. "See, right now, you look for all the world like no one looks at you."

"They don't. And that makes my job easy."

"That's a big fat lie, Perry." I point my glass at her. "I'm looking at you. I look at you a lot."

"You wouldn't if I didn't work for you."

"I don't know if that's true," I say.

But I take another sip of my drink, because I've a horrible feeling it might be true. But then again, would it? She commands attention. She draws the eye. She's smart, fun, and has a hot mouth, hotter body and a personality I could dive into for weeks on end. The better question would be if I'd ever be in the same place as her and I'm pretty sure the answer would be no.

"You're Ryder Sinclair and you know it. You use it. So stop trying to find an angle."

I place my hand on my heart. "Me?"

"You." She downs her drink and it's impressive. See? Layers. "Want to get out of here?"

"Hell yes," I say.

And that little invitation is all I need.

I get to my feet and take her hand and pull her up and against me.

And then I lean in to steal that kiss.

Chapter Fourteen

ELLIOT

My heart beats wild in my chest as my eyes flutter shut.

There's no pretending he isn't going to kiss me.

His gaze glittered with that intent as he pulled me to him, and I want that kiss more than my next breath.

The last time—the only time—we kissed buzzes in my veins and I'm just tingling with need, with desire and—

Oh shit. What am I doing?

I put a hand against his chest and open my eyes. He's so close, barely an inch from me and his mouth is oh so deliciously close.

"Ryder."

"What? I'm in the middle of something here, Elliot."

I want to melt. I force myself to keep solid form. "We can't."

"We can. It's easy. Very easy. We've done it before."

He's so close the warmth of his breath is on me and that intoxicating Ryder scent is invading every single cell of my body.

"I know," I say. "But I'm not kissing you."

"Why not?"

"Because..." Right now, I can't think of a reason. There are lots of reasons not to. I'm sure of it. I used to know them. But right now all I can think and breathe and want is him and that kiss, and my mind is telling me to run, but my body, my hormones are saying go for it, take that kiss.

"Because," I say again, "we should go. There's putting on a show and there's causing a scene."

"People kiss all the time, Perry. It's like a law or something."

I wish it was a law.

"No, I'm positive there's no law on this."

"Are you sure?"

"Yep. Checked all the books."

"What if I want to kiss you?"

I stare at him, my heart hammering, blood pressure shooting toward the roof. "Do you?"

Ryder Sinclair, the gorgeous asshole with the smile that can melt diamonds hesitates. Then he hesitates some more. When the hesitation continues, I want to kick myself. But instead, I decide to be the grown up. I step back from him.

"Stupid question," I say, turning.

Ryder grabs my arm. "Elliot..."

But I don't want this conversation in public, I don't want it in private. I don't want to be humiliated. I just smile a smile I don't feel because I'm a mess of emotions. A mess of relief, need, annoyance, lust.

"I just..." I stop. "Let's get out of here."

"Fine." He lets go of my arm and takes my hand again as we head toward the hostess table. He sends a text and then pays on his way out, handing the waitress a huge tip in cash.

I'm pretty sure she's willing to birth all his babies if he so much as asked.

Ryder collects our coats from the coat check, still holding my hand, and then we're outside, the coats draped over his arm.

He lets me go as he steps up to the curb where a shining black car waits and bundles me in.

I don't even ask where we're going because the moment the driver starts to head toward Houston Street, I know.

"Are you dropping me off, Ryder?"

"Hell no, I'm coming up." He looks at my face, then raises a brow. "You want to unleash me on the public?"

"Is this your form of blackmail slash torture?"

"People love spending time with me."

"Not all people, Ryder." Like me, because surely last night was enough torture.

"You did say we need to spend time together," he says, sounding smug and sure of himself.

Part of me wants to smack him down. Part of me wants to throw myself at him. And that's the problem. A man like him isn't what I want. A man like him is pure fantasy material.

I ignore the small voice that whispers how unexpectedly delightful he is. I do not need that voice. Instead, I remind myself what he's paying me and this is my job. "So you're saying you can't be trusted to be alone?"

"Yes, that's what I'm saying."

The car pulls up on the street near my building and I sigh. "Okay, come on up."

And his grin is pure decadence and delight.

As we head into my building, every cell in me jumping like live wires, I'm wondering what kind of sadist I am.

This man is dangerous. So very dangerous. To me. Because I'm so attracted to him it's sometimes hard to see straight. Or think straight.

My crush...it's huge. Full blown.

And yeah. He's really dangerous.

Inside my apartment, he makes himself at home, getting drinks for us, putting music on by hooking up his phone to the Bluetooth sound system I have.

I kick off my heels and take the whiskey on the rocks he holds out, and sip it, to give myself something to do that doesn't involve me either running and hiding or ripping his clothes off.

Clearly, I have problems.

So does Ryder Sinclair.

Because he's looking at me with smolder in those melting chocolate eyes and I'm buzzing. The music doesn't help, either. It's sultry and low, easy and seductive.

"You like this kind of music?" I ask.

It's old school, like really old school, bluesy, jazzy, from when life was dressing to the nines and films came in black and white and bigger than life with the impossible glamor.

"Since I have it, I'm going to hazard the answer to that is yes, Perry."

"Interesting."

"What?" He gives his head a small shake before sprawling on the sofa. "I can't have taste?"

"I don't know, can you?"

"I like you. Does that count as taste, Perry?" He grins as he picks up his drink. "Don't sell yourself short or I'll put on some autotuned pop."

"That," I say, "sounds more like you."

"That sounds suspiciously like an insult."

"Take it how you want." I set my drink on the coffee table. "I'm getting changed."

His gaze slides over me. "I didn't bring anything for myself."

"I have some Hello Kitty pajamas you can wear."

"Or I can wear nothing at all..."

Heat pools inside me and that familiar tingling down in my sex starts. I open my mouth but I can't think of a damned word to say that isn't along the line of take me now, so I turn and scurry off to my room.

Inside, I lean against the closed door, shutting my eyes and my legs start to shake.

Oh, man. He's beyond dangerous. He's a secret weapon. And I don't know what to do.

It isn't even that he wants me. I'm aware enough that he's the kind of low-down man whore who'd do any woman he found mildly attractive. But he turned my act of dressing down into some sort of flirt fest and—

I need to get my shit together. That's what I need to do.

Taking in a breath, I straighten up and open my eyes. Then I strip down and find pajamas, this time the old man style of thick stripes and a long sleeved button down top, all in that unsexiest of materials, flannel. Then I head to my bathroom, scrape my hair back and remove the bare minimum make up.

And okay, I feel a little silly for doing this like I'm some femme fatale or pin up girl, but it's more for me than for him.

When I finally emerge and head back, the lamps are on, the overhead off, and Ryder looks for all the world like he's settled in and made himself at home. His shoes and socks are off, his jacket and waistcoat and tie abandoned; and that dark head with the soft loose curls is bent over a book.

The image slams me hard against the floor, smacking me in the solar plexus. Because like that, he's the picture of my dream man.

I've got it bad and I need to stop.

I sit on the other end of the sofa and pick up my drink from where he's placed it, on a coaster on the coffee table, and I hold it like it's some kind of lifeline to reality and good sense.

He finishes the page he's on, slides a finger down between that and the next one and turns it. Finally, he glances at me. "Really?"

"What?" I frown.

He waves the book in my general direction before closing it and setting it down. Ryder crosses his legs. "The hair, the old dude at the homeless shelter vibe pajamas, you know."

I pull my legs up beneath my chin and shoot him a look. "How do you know that's not the look I was going for?"

"I'm pretty sure you were." He leans forward. "If I was so inclined, this wouldn't stop me making a move. It's sexy in its own way. Except the hair. That makes you look like a librarian. Actually, I take that back, because librarian fantas—"

"Please." I push the book and him away. "Of course you have a librarian fantasy. If it's female, you've got a fantasy."

He shrugs. "Is that a problem?"

"Ryder, yes. You have to get this shit under control." His mother's words come back to me, and the purpose of why he's here, why he hired me. Not to mention the fact he's flirting like it's breathing and my hormones are in overdrive, acting like the worst kind of naïve, acting like he means it.

I'm not his type. I don't want to be his type. Spending hours on hair and make-up and clothes and appealing to a man bores me. Take me or leave me has always been my motto. So why does this one affect me so much?

The stupid physical crush, that's what it is.

"I'm not going to do anything," he says.

"Because I'm not your type, unless you class female as a type."

He shoots me a low-lidded look, then sets down the book and picks up his drink. "You think I'm immune to you?"

"What does that even mean?"

"That you don't affect me."

I sigh. "Ryder, you're saying this because I'm the only female near you. The only one you can have any kind of...one-on-one contact with for the rest of the month. Now, since you're here, we need to talk about those plans."

"Shifting the subject?"

"This is the only one we're discussing."

"Not why your toenails are siren red, but your fingernails are beige boredom?"

I'm not going to laugh. "They're a very light pink."

"That's even worse."

I snatch up my drink and hold it. "It's the sort of color that goes with anything. I work for a living."

"So do I."

"What I mean is," I say, taking a swallow of the cool whiskey, "is I have to present in a certain way."

"Is frump a certain way?"

I just stare at him. "I'm a frump who wears old homeless man pajamas? Sinclair, keep this up and I'll be putty in your hands."

Ryder starts to laugh. "Jesus, Elliot. I wouldn't even call a frump a frump, I'm not that into death wishes. And I don't think there are frumps, just clothes that don't show off assets how they should and how the fuck do you do this to me?"

"Do what?"

"Tie my words into knots?" He slides across to me and my breath is caught in my throat as he reaches out, touching my hair. "I'm good with women. Very good."

"Or very bad."

"Sometimes," he says, with a small smile as he pulls the band from my hair and rakes his finger through it, making me shiver with pleasure from the sudden release of the pull, and from the soft slide of his fingers against my scalp and then down through my hair, "sometimes, that's the exact same thing."

"Maybe it's because I'm not falling over myself to please you, and maybe I'm not impressed."

"Maybe," he says. "And maybe I like a challenge."

The electrified taunt in his words is full of sensual innuendo and my stomach flip-flops. "In a few weeks, you'll be able to impress all the women your trashy heart desires and you won't even have to try."

"Trashy?" He winces.

"Trashy."

Now he slides his hand down along my cheekbone. "I'm not trashy. And how is this about me? I'm talking about you."

"I'm a boring subject," I say, going to push his hand away, but instead he turns it on me and links our fingers. "Stop that."

"Stop what?"

"The flirting."

"Friendly flirting," he says. "I'm natural born. I don't even color it. And what the fuck's wrong with a little flirting?"

"Oh, you know the jewels, the company you want to remain in your family. The big change you have to do."

"Appear to do."

I take in a breath, but I can't tell him what his mother said to me. I don't even know what she was trying to get at with it beyond her general warning. "Sometimes you have to give a little, bring that change into you, to make it believable."

"That's your job and you're changing the subject." Suddenly, he points a finger at me. "You don't like flirting because it puts the attention on you."

"No. I don't like stupid flirting when there's nothing behind it."

He lifts the corner of his mouth. "But that's ridiculous. Flirting is like air. It's what keeps you alive and it's good. Also, flirting is just what you said."

"So you admit it's empty?" I ask. "With nothing behind it."

Ryder doesn't speak for a moment. "Not what I said. Look at it like shopping."

"I'm not into shopping."

But he ignores me as he looks around my apartment and back at me.

"You know what I mean, Sinclair. Not into the boutiques. Not into having to spend my money to feel good. There's window shopping, and there's seeing something and going for it. Flirting is window shopping. Sometimes it's just for fun and then you see what you like, really like, and it morphs."

"Flirting is a transformer?"

"I don't know what you're talking about." He's still got my hand, I realize, our fingers linked. Ryder points at me again with his free hand. "And you're wiggling out. You don't like the attention on you."

"I don't get attention. I'm not you."

He frowns. "Only because you choose not to. You hide, and I bet you like to reflect the attention. I'm betting you've done this so long you don't realize it. I bet you did that growing up."

"That's a lot of bets." But his words make something ring out in me.

"I'd win them all. You reflect by nurturing. It's in your company, it's in how you operate, in how you choose beautiful old things, and it's in your plants. And I bet if I asked, you were one of those nurturer kids. See, that way you can hide and feel good."

"That's bullshit."

"Is it? I think I'm right. You hide and you try to blend in."

"I do blend in—"

"Because you work at it. And it's so ingrained you don't know you're doing it."

My mouth is dry. This is all utter crap...isn't it? "Save me from your amateur hour sofa therapy."

"Hey, I charge a fortune for this. How do you think I got so rich?"

I shake off his hand and lift my fingers to my cheek and tap it. "Hmmm, I'm thinking either you stole it or inherited it."

"Now you're trying to deflect. I think you should let yourself shine."

"I'm not a shiner. I'm a lurker. I do well in the shadows, way out of the limelight. Shining and the rest? That's not me."

"It could be, if you let it, Perry."

"And what do you know?"

"A lot," Ryder says softly.

He slides closer, his hand skimming along my thigh and that heat crackles like lightning between us again, the air thick with awareness and he's close, so close.

"This might be easy for you, Ryder," I say, wanting to run, wanting to throw caution to the wind and kiss him, "like breathing. But not for me."

"What? Wanting to kiss you?"

"Flirting."

"I'm not flirting." His gaze drops to my lips. "I like your mouth."

Suddenly I lose that battle and I surge up and I kiss him.

Ryder takes that and runs, his mouth is hot and wet and beguiling, it seduces, it doesn't demand, and I give back, my lips parting, our tongues touching. It's a flame that devours slowly and I'm losing everything to the heat inside, the heat he causes.

It's not until his hand slides against the bare flesh of my ribcage that I come crashing down.

I tear my mouth aside. "No, Ryder. You're doing this because I'm the only one around."

"You kissed me, Elliot."

"You can't have me. This was a dumb idea."

He sits back, sliding his hand through his hair and he says, "I thought it was a great idea."

"You and me? There's no you and me. You're not into me and we're not like that."

"I know—"

"I think I'm going to go to bed." I'm on my feet so fast it's a wonder I don't have whiplash. And then, before he can shake off the surprise on his face, I turn and race off to my room.

There, I shut the door, turn off the light, and just dive into bed.

Maybe he wasn't saying he knows he's not into me. And maybe I ran like a scared little girl.

But I had to.

I'm an idiot and crushing way too hard and kissing him was the most stupid thing I could do.

Coming out of this in one piece isn't a matter of dealing with a bruised ego from an unrequited crush. It's something else.

Because Ryder Sinclair isn't just a fuck boy with a pretty face and a mouth that can kiss. He's smart. He's funny. He's fun. He's deeper and way more complex than I'd ever given him credit for.

I'm lost and I don't know anything.
Except for one thing.
Oh boy, am I in major trouble.

Chapter Fifteen

Ryder

The first big meeting with the board went well and things are good. I've been busy, but not too busy to lose track of my goals. Everything I want is there, just in reach. All I need is to get through the next three weeks.

Get through them and a little time after, because I'm not stupid, and I'll be golden. I know my mother, and my father, and I wouldn't put it past him to have built in some weird clause as each step for me and my brothers keeps getting more intricate with more at stake; and my mother because she's a sneaky woman and is not only carrying out dear old father's ghostly orders but has her own agenda.

The stakes keep climbing and I don't know why. But what I want keeps me grounded, focused.

I just need to behave for the next handful of weeks.

It's why I have Elliot.

After the meeting I head home and work from there because I have fewer distractions there.

I don't even realize I'm running late to Mag's place for drinks—the one thing he and Zoey haven't yet worked out is where they're living, so they split time between his place and hers above her store, which makes me laugh, thinking of my ruthless brother in such small digs.

Then again, there's nothing to laugh about, not really. They're disgustingly happy, just like Scarlett and Hud.

My phone rings and something lights up in me when I see Elliot's name. "You're late," I say, closing down my computer and pushing back my chair.

She laughs softly, that low sexy voice with the smoky depths washes through me. Without her there I can immerse in it. The woman should make recordings. "Nice greeting, Sinclair."

"I try."

But the laughter stops.

"Ryder, I'm sorry, I can't make it. I've some work and—"

"With what I'm paying, how the hell do you fit anyone else in?"

"For you, idiot," she says, "but I have an unexpected family thing I can't get out of."

The light sinks. "Not a problem."

We ring off and I don't know why it leaves me feeling a little empty. Probably because my cager is also a crutch. I can trust Elliot to keep me on the straight and narrow. Not that I've had time for anything else. And tonight's it's drinks with my brothers. They want to know how the meeting went.

So I head on out.

I'm a grown man. I can do this myself.

I have drinks with my brothers and their significant others, and we discuss the meeting. There's nothing much, no giant signs about what's going on, but the word on the street, or boardroom as it were, is they're happy.

The board and my brothers? They're just intrigued and King wants the money. He's got plans but he won't really discuss them as he has to head out early to take care of shit in his business life, and me? I'm fucking tired. So I make my goodbyes.

"You all right?" Magnus asks as he walks me to his door. "It's not the bet is it?"

I give him a filthy look. "You guys are still doing that?"

"Of course. And you know the stakes are going to rise since your Elliot didn't show. You didn't sleep with her, did you?"

"No, I did not."

"That unattractive?"

My hand curls into a fist and my brother's gaze drops to it and he grins.

"Oh, God," I say. "You have a side bet on that, don't you?"

He shrugs. "Come on. It's fucking you. And while she doesn't come across all flash and tits and sex, she's passable."

"Elliot has something you don't understand. Class. I mean, sure, you're marrying class, but you're an asshole and you don't get it. I don't know what Zoey sees in you."

"My brilliance."

"You lied to her."

"Water under the bridge." He waves a hand. "And we're not talking about me, we're talking about you. Namely, have you nailed her yet?"

"Don't talk about Elliot that way, and I answered."

"You talk about women like that all the time."

I just shake my head and leave.

Seriously, me? Talk about women that way? I'm pretty sure I have more imagination than that.

I get in the car service I called. The night is mine, I realize. Mine to do with how I see fit and as I head home, I'm aware there are too many bars and clubs and places to be. And trouble to get into.

I'm tired but now I'm feeling restless. A drink somewhere dark and anonymous appeals and I can do it. Right? I'm sure I can.

But the closer we head to TriBeCa the more people are out and about and the more I begin to not trust myself.

It's been a little bit since I've had sex. And more than a week is a hell of a long time. It's like dying of thirst.

I've got too much riding on all this for me to slip up. I lean forward. "A change of plans," I say to the driver. "Prince Street."

Elliot buzzes me in. She looks soft and sweet, her hair pinned back but in a looser style, with red locks escaping. She's in a pretty enough dress and has one low heel in a hand. "Don't tell me you were tempted."

As a greeting goes, it's not the best, but it could be worse. I close the door and lean against it and fold my arms. I'm in jeans and a cashmere sweater, as it's warmer tonight.

"Okay, I won't."

Thing is we've spent other nights together since those first two. The rest at my place where she had her own room. For some reason, I prefer this.

Elliot takes off her other shoe and sets them down. "Well, at least you came to the temptation-free temple."

"I wouldn't say that."

She just shakes her head and sits on the sofa, rubbing her feet. "You're incorrigible."

"How about I get us a drink and do that for you and you can tell me all about your day." I don't give her a chance to argue. Instead, I go to the kitchen—I know my way about the small space by now—and pour some whiskeys. Then I hand one to her, take a sip of mine, then set it on the coffee table and sit.

I ease her feet into my lap and start to massage them. She makes a surprisingly erotic sound in her throat as I do so.

Elliot has surprisingly pretty feet. They're long, elegant, delicate, and there's something intimate about what I'm doing. I look up and she's got her lip caught between her teeth, eyes closed as she leans back, one hand clasped about her glass, the other gripping the sofa.

Fuck. My cock stirs and I make sure her feet are nowhere in that vicinity.

I shouldn't be turned on, but who wouldn't be at that sight? It's orgasmic, the pleasure of my touch an electric beacon in her and that turns me on. The fact I'm doing that to her, just by touching her feet is hot.

And maybe part of it is her seeming lack of interest in me. I say seeming because, damn it, she kissed me the other night.

Then she ran away.

Still, it's a little disconcerting to have her rebuff me every time I try and compliment her. It doesn't help I keep getting things wrong when I do that.

I shove it all away. I like women. End of story.

"Well?"

She opens an eye. "Well what?"

"Your day? Your evening?"

"Work. For you. And don't worry, no splashy articles or interviews or declarations of love or the new your kinda deal. It's just all the boring mechanics of making sure what is out there or will be is tweaked our way. And you've been behaving."

"I mostly do," I say, ignoring all the times I don't. "Also I've been busy."

"And I haven't let you spend the night alone." She opens her other eye and takes a sip of her drink, making no move to pull her feet free.

"I'm not a total lost cause."

"The jury is still out."

"It's a bogus jury."

She laughs. "The evening wasn't exciting. Just being the dutiful daughter for my great aunt's eighty-sixth birthday. I forgot." Elliot glances down into her glass, the light from the lamps making her hair gleam. "I've had a lot on my mind."

"Me."

"Don't make yourself more important than you are."

I rest my hand on top of her feet and pick up my glass. "Perry, that was cold."

"That's me. I'm like ice."

"I'm thinking more like there's a river of lava in there, not ice."

She shifts and pulls her feet off me, but rests them against my thigh. I like the heat and the pressure. "What are you going to do if we can't pull this off?"

"By that, you mean me."

I take a swallow of the drink.

She sighs. "Ryder, I only meant—"

"I know what you meant." I say this quietly. "If I fuck up by fucking someone inappropriate. By doing something they don't like. By being me."

"Ryder—"

"I like me," I say. "I've told you this shit shouldn't matter."

"But it does, because you deemed it so."

I take another swallow of the amber liquid. "Because it's a connection to my past, my heritage, like I told you. And the company means something. I fucking hate the fact the stakes keep growing since this all started, and I don't want to lose it."

I stop and meet her gaze.

"Thing is, Elliot, it means more to me than the others. It's part of me, you know? The others, they see it as our heritage, too. And no one wants it to go public, and I can't be the catalyst for that."

"You don't want to be the fuck up."

"I know what people think of me. Eternal playboy, the guy who likes fun and fucking women more than anything else, and maybe they're right. Life is short. It's there to enjoy when you can. But I'm more than that. I made my own fortune. This...the jewels...they were always talked about as a symbol of the Sinclair name. And to me, as a kid, they seemed impossible. I believed in them, always, and now they've turned up, I want mine."

She nods and sips her drink. "The legendary value? The monetary value? Are they important? You can't wear them."

"I think I could pull it off." I slide my hand over the silk of her calf, her skin smooth and warm beneath my palm. "There's a romance to them, a history I want to know. I want to see them all together. I know they were made as a gift for my great grandmother. And...it's like how you love all these art deco pieces. They're beautiful. The two pieces I've seen are that, beautiful. I want to see them all."

"You haven't seen them?"

"No. There aren't pictures, they're rumors. Stories. Lore. And that's worth more. That, and not being the fuck up who ruins the family company."

She doesn't respond for a long time, but finally she says, "There's a lot more to you, Ryder. And we can do this." Elliot stops, and her gaze catches mine and it burns, making something twist deep inside me. "You can."

"I got you." I grin at her and she turns red and returns her gaze to her drink. "Ryder."

"Hey." I wait until that pretty and vulnerable and fierce gaze returns to me. "It's true. I don't know if I can do this without you. It's nice, you know? Having someone in my corner."

"Even if you're paying them." She lifts her drink and takes a sip.

"Even that. And you're right, I can do this." I'm not sure if I'm telling a lie with that, because pretty is pretty and need is need and I'm not used to denying myself. All it would take is a slip... "But you help me. More than just hiring you. I don't want to lose the company, my connection to the past, to my family's history."

"You can do anything you want, Ryder, even get your urges under control. If urges is the right word," she says. "I'm here to guide and rebuild your image in a subtle way that backs up what you do. After you get what you want, you have to decide what you're going to do."

"Yeah, well, conservative and staid and picket fences aren't me and they're never gonna be me. I like freedom. I like thrills. I also like hard work. And this whole thing is stupid, but I'll do it." I sigh and rest my hand against her feet. The connection soothes and riles all at the same time, all in a good way. "Short answer is I'll find a way."

"It's only a few weeks, then you can get back to your hot women."

"I have one here."

She raises a brow. "That's a little rude, sneaking one in."

"There you go again." I give her a contemplative look. "Deflecting the soft flirt, the attention."

"You don't mean it and I don't like it."

"Which part? Flirting or attention? I know you hide, and I told you why I think you do it, but what happened?"

"There are a lot of us who let the others shine. They like that light, like you. I don't. And people...they don't see me because they expect the flash and dazzle. I'm not that. I'm good behind the scenes and I'm good at guiding and fixing and that's why I'm excellent at what I do."

"Bullshit."

"Excuse me, Sinclair?"

My skin starts to heat. I don't know how she does it, how she gets me in knots when usually I'm smooth as silk. "I know you're the best at what you do, otherwise I wouldn't have hired you. I just mean it's bullshit about not being seen. I see you."

Elliot sighs. "Only because I'm working with you. You'd never give someone like me the time of day, otherwise. And I'm not complaining. Things are as they are, that's all."

"Of course I would," I say. "I don't discriminate, I told you that."

"Being a man whore isn't the same as seeing someone for their worth, Ryder."

Her words strike some place deep inside me. "Maybe I wasn't talking about sex for sex's sake there, Perry." I drag in a breath because that thing inside hurts. Not for me. For her. I somehow hurt her and I don't know how or why.

"Really?"

"You know, I've never had a female friend. They usually want something from me, which is fine, I usually want something from them. But you...you don't want anything from me, and I enjoy spending time with you. I've never met anyone like you before, Elliot. Not once in my life and I think I'd have seen you. And maybe there's more to it."

"Ryder."

I ignore the warning because I want to see if the sweet, evocative taste of her is everywhere. I want to see where this goes. I want her.

I set my drink down and take hers, moving up over her and looking down. Her eyes are big and dilated and that need and want that flashes in them transforms her somehow.

"Sex," I say, "can be all sorts of things."

I lean down to kiss her, but her hand comes up on my chest and my heart's beating hard and fast and uneven.

"It's not a good idea, Ryder."

"Why? I think there's chemistry here, begging to be explored."

But Elliot pushes me and I fall back. "No, it's because you need a woman, Ryder, but I'm not willing to just be a notch or to fill in until something better comes along."

"That's not fair."

"Who said life is? You have a hand. I have a bathroom. Make yourself at home."

I stare at her and shake my head. "You want me to jerk off?"

"If that helps," she says evenly as she gets to her feet. "I—you know where all the bedding is. Goodnight."

And just like that, Elliot turns and walks away.

Chapter Sixteen

ELLIOT

Oh my God.

I just suggested he go rub one out in my bathroom.

What the actual fuck is wrong with me?

The man also was about to make a move and I pushed him away...

Okay, okay, I get that one, because it's going to end in hurt, a world of it, for me if I kiss him again and it wouldn't have been a kiss. It would have been a whole lot more and he makes me... He makes me feel alive.

Even though he never says the right thing. I don't know why, and I don't know what this is, except I want it from him. And I'm more than aware he wants me because he can't have someone else. Anyone else. Hell, it might be built into his DNA to hit on a woman. I don't know.

That hurts, but it also rocks my foundations a little.

Makes me unsure of myself. Which is ludicrous.

I'm confident. I know my place—I like my place. I like the shadows and staying there. I like quiet affairs of the heart with someone smart and level and who treats me with respect. I'm not unwanted, I've had partners, relationships. I've had men want me, and yes, I've turned men down.

But never one like Ryder.

I'm shaking, and I sink down to the floor, leaning my head back against the door.

Bottom line is it doesn't matter if he wants me for me or because I'm a warm body whose mind he likes. If I let him, if he did it right, if he turned that Ryder on, the one who is so smooth and electrifying, I know he'd have me naked in moments.

No. I'd have me naked in moments. No matter what he meant, if anything at all.

And I hate that weakness.

I'm not weak.

Except when it comes to him.

How the hell am I going to get through the next three weeks?

Because I was dealing with the microcosms that keep cropping up when it comes to him. His scandal couldn't have come at a worse time for him. Because the couple involved are famous. Worse, they're hungry for it, and whether their marriage is real or fake, or over privately, in the papers and magazines and online it's not. Opinion sways. That's one reason I created the relationship for him with me.

That way I can control it. Sure, I tried to find someone, but this is better—for him.

But the way he looks, his history, his wealth, it's all catnip to the paps. And he could spend a year as a monk and one article could keep him from reaching his goals. So I've got things in motion.

A soft tapping at my door draws me from my thoughts.

"Elliot?"

Crap. He's all I need. The questioning tone I need even less. Because it's vulnerable and confused and... And how does he do that? Flip the script?

I'm not even sure that's what he's doing, but it feels like it because he's hotter than the sun and I'm...I'm me.

Someone who doesn't fall for his kind. Ever.

Yet here I am. Hiding.

"Yes?"

"Can you open the door?"

I push myself up the door and put my hand on the knob but stop, leaning my forehead against the wood. "I don't think that's smart."

He's silent a long time and I'm half hoping he's given up. But finally, he speaks. "Did I do something wrong?"

"Yes. No. Nothing. Everything. It doesn't matter."

"It does. You took off."

"Ryder..." Thing is, he doesn't get it, doesn't see that something he does like he takes his next breath is huge for me. And asking if he did something wrong, I just...it's all jagged and sharp edged. Because would he ask someone else? I can't shake that feeling he wouldn't have tried something if we weren't in this situation. If he wasn't in this situation. And that makes me stupid and weak and all the things I dislike.

"Ryder," I say again, "you're my client."

"So?"

I breathe out, wanting desperately to turn that knob. Wanting to step out and just go with whatever happens.

"So, we belong in two different worlds. You like the limelight. I hate it. You...you don't do relationships and I do. We're working together."

"You know, Elliot," he says, his voice soft and close like he's leaning against the door on the other side, and the silly part of me can almost feel him there, that vibrating awareness, that pull. "I get it."

"You do?"

"Yeah. You're not into me. You don't see me that way."

I'm going to regret my next question. "What way?"

"Like I'm long term. Like you want something deep and romantic with me."

He has no idea and my hand starts to turn the knob when he speaks again.

"And that's okay. It's not me. I'm not that guy. But I like you. I'm attracted to you and there's something between us. I'm not an idiot and this is one area where I'm pretty much a fucking genius, so I know you feel the same, and you feel that awareness. So, I don't know. Friends with benefits."

My hand slides to the lock and I click it into place.

I don't want him coming in here again.

"Good night, Ryder."

And with that, I go to bed.

My work schedule is complicated. Ryder is complicated. I try not to think about that night a handful of days ago, but it's hard. I could have had him. Could have thrown caution to the wind and accepted that offer.

A one-night stand? They happen. Nights of passion that go nowhere except into friendship? They happen. And relationships, too. I'm no stranger to any of those things. But I don't do friends with benefits.

I'm not against it. It's just not a scenario I can see myself fitting into. If I make room for someone, I want a relationship. I want them to want me the way I do them—all of them. And Ryder Sinclair doesn't give his all to anyone.

Oh, in the moment, I'm sure. And—

Nope. I'm definitely not going to imagine him having sex and what it's like.

Instead, I go back to my complicated micromanaging and molding of Ryder.

Maybe that's all it is. I have to spend all my time with a hot man. It's no wonder I'm crushing hard, no wonder I want him. I'm immersed in him.

Problem is, I thought the longer I spent doing this, the weaker the attraction would get. But he's more than he seems on paper. And every layer is intriguing. Both the good and the bad.

The last two nights I needed a break. And I also needed to spend time working out our next phase.

And just like some kind of kid with burning ears, Ryder arrives in my office. Without knocking.

"No one was at the desk, so I came on in."

"It's almost seven, Ryder, and my receptionist has a life."

There's a half smile on his face. I know why. Lena is hot and just his type and she's told me all about her fantasies about him. He's probably got similar ones to hers.

"Pity. She seems...nice."

I narrow my eyes. "She's off limits to you."

"Hey, I just said she seemed nice, not that I wanted to bone her."

"But you would."

"I'm pleading the fifth. Besides..." His gaze slides over me in my suit. "I like you."

I finish up, grab my bag and coat, and we head out into the SoHo night.

As we head to an upscale bar on Orchard Street, I give him a low glance. We find a table—Ryder can always get a table—and settle in. "Drinks are the plan?"

He's ordered drinks and fries. The drinks arrive in short notice, just gin and tonic for me and a mescal on the rocks for him, and he sets his gaze on me. Waiting.

I shrug. "No one's going to buy it if you just go out to galas and work events, or just see your brothers or we stay in. You go out. So we go out."

"And you let me choose?"

I shrug again. "You have taste, Ryder, and this is a nice bar."

The fries arrive and he takes one, and Lord do they smell good, they're lightly spiced with smoked paprika from the earthy, sweet scent that carries that rich hit of smoke, so I take one, too, and moan.

"Jesus," he mutters, eating his. "They're good, but not that good. Or is that erotic sound you're making for my benefit? Because I gotta tell you, Perry, you don't need to up that game to hook me."

"They're that good. Not everything's about you."

I forgot to have lunch today so the fries are perfect, and heat coils and licks within me at his words, and the gin just gives the heat a boost.

He laughs. "Are you sure? Because the latest Ryder Sinclair Weekly mag came out, and it said I was."

"You have problems."

"Nope, it also says I'm pretty much perfect."

"Do not—" I shake a fry at him "—make me launch these at you. They're too good."

"If I'd known this is what it would take to get you making hot sounds, I'd have been feeding you fries from Basic since day one. What else gets you going?"

"Idiot." This time I do throw one at him. Ryder catches it and eats it. "I'm going to the bathroom. Try not to get into trouble."

"Me? Never."

I head off, and after I use the facility I take my time washing my hands so I can think. Ryder's a little softer now, more relaxed in his role.

The other night, I was too caught up in the moment to see it, but I think he really can pull this off. He's chosen a place that's him but not flash and sizzle.

It's not full of models and the kind of hot women he's photographed with. This isn't even the kind of place that draws the attention of the paps.

It's neighborhood, happening and upscale, yes, but it's small, too.

Even his flirting with me is more laid back. I don't think he'll ever stop that. I think flirting is as much a part of Ryder as his charm. But he's not angling for anything like he was the other night. Oh, he made the comments about the erotic sounds, but that's Ryder, right?

And I know he likes me, likes spending time with me. But that's neither here nor there. This is about him and the change in him.

Maybe it's real, maybe it's an act, but if it's an act then he's doing a stellar job. I buy it, and if I do, then the board and his mother might too.

Who knows, if it's an act, it's one that comes from a place of sincerity, not cynicism. And that means real change, if he wants it, can happen. What's that line? Fake it till you make it?

There's a lightness to my step as I turn to leave. But it thumps down the moment I step out into the back hall of the bar. A woman stands in front of the single occupant bathroom and she blocks my path. Someone else starts to ask about the bathroom, but she waves them past.

She's looking at me, her beautiful face cool and narrow-eyed.

There's no need to ask. Ryder slept with her at some point. She has that look and she's up his alley.

"Can I help you?" I ask.

Her gaze travels over me and her perfect nose wrinkles, her mouth twisting in a delicate sneer. "Have his standards fallen so far?"

"Obviously, I can't, so if you'll excuse me, I have my boyfriend to get back to."

The word feels so weird, so alien, as I say it. Normally I'd never go there, and I know she's not media of any kind, not officially, but there's social media and for the next few weeks I'm watching my mouth because anything I say that's used online can be way more powerful than an article.

But the word is a trigger and the woman's face turns ugly with hate. "Boyfriend? Maybe, but you've got to have something on him. And trust me, a man like Ryder Sinclair, who looks like that, will never in a million years be faithful to someone like you."

"Or maybe he knows real quality when he sees it." Inside I'm shaking. But not on the outside.

Even if Ryder was mine, I'd never give trash like this the satisfaction. And this isn't unexpected. She thinks I have something she couldn't get looking like her—Ryder. As in basically living with him. Going out with him. Sure, she slept with him, but that isn't the same as a relationship.

Not that I have him, but she thinks that.

It's almost laughable. But I don't make that mistake.

"You're not quality—"

"Maybe not. But Ryder thinks so."

And without another word, I step around her and head back into the main part of the bar.

Our table is empty.

With a sinking heart and a flash of something hot and jagged-edged, I see Ryder. At the bar.

In conversation with a gorgeous blonde in a low-cut top and painted on black shiny jeans.

Oh, hell no.

His hand is on her hip and she's giving him the sex eyes.

I don't think. I just do.

I march over there. Time to break it up.

"What the fuck are you doing?" I demand.

And Ryder's dark gaze swings to me.

Chapter Seventeen

RYDER

It's like all the shit hits the fan and for once I've done nothing wrong.

Because I haven't done anything except go to get some drinks from the bar. It's not my fault the grabby blonde took one look at me and latched on with her fake nails.

I expect her to slink away, but she doesn't and Elliot taps her fingers against her arm. "Well?"

I offer Elliot my best smile, but I might well have not for all it did me. Nothing melted in her. Not even a hint.

Damn, but I like her, and the worst part is I can hear the disappointment when she speaks. She's the last person I want to disappoint. After all, we're friends. At least, I think we're friends.

Even if she's harboring murderous thoughts.

"I'm just talking, Elliot," I say, "you know how it is."

"No, I don't, but I'm beginning to. Are you going to introduce me to your friend, Ryder?"

"Oh." Shit. I desperately try to remember the name of the very hot, octopus-like woman who, for some reason, is still there, still a little too close, but I can't. "We were just chatting."

The fire in Elliot's gaze is fierce and the woman slides in closer to me and I realize with horror I have my hand on her.

I'd put it there to stop her getting closer, and rebuffing women is a skill I seem to have lost, apparently. I used to be able to do it with ease, without thinking, but I'm trying to be someone I'm not, and that skill goes hand in hand with picking up the woman of the moment.

Not that I'd have picked up this blonde. But under normal circumstances, I'd have shut it all down so smoothly I wouldn't be in this situation. Trying to be noble is utter shit, if you ask me. So is being sincerely nice. Or trying to be sincerely nice. It gets you into trouble with certain tall redheads and means you can't smoothly repel cheap, hot blondes.

Elliot is glaring like this thing with us is real and there's something about that. It gets to me, winds down deep against my bones.

"Really?"

"Back off, bitch." The woman's hotness points drop way down to the single digit area with this. "I think he's done with you."

"I think you should watch your mouth," Elliot says before I can say a word as I start to rise from the bar stool I took waiting to be served.

The woman tosses her hair and it almost hits me in the face. "I think you should find something your own level."

"That's no way to talk to her," I say quietly as I disentangle the woman who's now below the single digit line and into the negative.

"You've got me now," the woman says, fluttering eyelashes up at me.

Elliot rolls her eyes. "Yes, you've got her now. Lucky you."

"We were just talking, that's it."

"Really?"

"Stop saying really." I decide to push it a little more. I don't like looking like an ass if I'm turning someone down and this blonde is making me be one. I didn't come looking for her, and I didn't encourage her—so I use the opportunity for myself. "Thing is, I just came to get us some drinks, but..." I swing my gaze from Elliot to the woman. "After your lovely insults, I think my fiancée and I are going to head home."

The woman doesn't look bothered at all by what I said to her.

"If you change your mind, here's my card." And the blonde hands me an actual card, embossed with the logo of a prestigious law firm I immediately make a priority not to work with.

Elliot takes the card. "Come on, lover-boy, time to get out of here."

I pay up and when I turn, Elliot's nowhere to be seen. The blonde's sidling up again, but I excuse myself and make my way out of the bar and to the pavement, where Elliot's standing, wrapped in her coat, impatience all over her.

"Really?"

I stare at her, guilt swamping me for something I didn't do. "Are we going to have our first fight as a happy couple?"

"No." She snaps the word, that rich voice low. "We've fought before."

"For the show."

Elliot stalks up to me, ignoring the people around us and grabs me by my suit jacket. She pulls me in close and I go. "You keep fucking up."

"Oh, do tell."

"You were all over a blonde, for one."

"I think you'll find she was all over me."

Elliot nods and looks up at me, eyes glittering. "Story of your life, huh?"

"A bit. But I went to get us another round and she started talking."

"You are pathetic," she says.

"Jealous?"

Her eyes are now slits. "Of that? No. If you want her, go get her. Go get the other and have round three or four or whatever."

"You sure sound jealous."

"I don't think your ego needs any inflating. I'm working for you. And I can quit, Ryder. Ever think of that?"

That sends a cold shard of ice through me. "You wouldn't."

"I will if you keep screwing around, if you keep causing waves."

"And what the fuck did I cause? I went to get us drinks. The server was busy, so I thought I'd be nice—"

"And hit on a woman?"

"Fuck, Elliot. What is it you want from me? I can't stop people talking to me. And I'm not going to. That's weird. It would be nice for once to have you in my corner."

"I am."

"And believe me."

She breathes out.

"Yeah, thought so," I say.

"Trust needs to be earned."

"How have I made you not trust me? I haven't fucked anyone since all this started. And—"

"Ryder." Her voice is still low, but now censure has joined in with the snark. "You have something you're paying me to do and yet here you are, sabotaging. You might not think you aren't, but you are. You just keep on flirting and doing you. And guess what? That's not going to get you what you want."

"I also can't be someone I'm not."

"But you have to change. Or seem to."

"I'm paying you—"

"You have to do the work, Ryder. Do you want to prove you've changed? Because even pretend change doesn't involve you chatting up some blonde babe while out on a date."

Frustration threatens to swamp me. The girl came up to me, came on to me. I didn't cause a scandal. I didn't do anything. And Elliot keeps upping her ante. She keeps making things harder. She keeps pushing.

"I told her I was with someone. And I damn well called you my fiancée."

"Ryder—"

"You were there. I told her I was with my fiancée."

She clicks her tongue. "Why would you do that? I don't understand."

"I thought it would be a good buffer. I thought—"

"Pity you can't be your own buffer. Do that yourself. You know, with your mouth and your actions."

"I was being smooth."

"No." She glares at me. "I've been insulted by two women tonight in there. One you fucked, the other you would be probably fucking now if I hadn't come up, and I can't always be there. You need to be able to keep it under wraps, Ryder."

What the hell's she talking about? Two women? The blonde was an idiot, and was rude, but... "What do you mean, two?"

"I was accosted in the bathroom by some woman."

"How is that my fault? I didn't set anyone on you."

She slides a little closer to me and drops her voice a little more and I can't stop myself from placing my hands on her hips, tugging her closer so she's flush against me. I'm telling myself it's for the game, for the show, but she feels good. She's warm and soft and right and if I keep going along this line of thought, I'm going to end up with a raging hard on.

"You slept with her. That much was obvious."

"I don't hand out special markers, Perry, so how is it obvious?"

Elliot lets out a frustrated sound. "Because she's your type. Like the blonde."

"Maybe," I say, "I did sleep with the other woman, but stop with the type thing. I like women. I've fucked a lot of them. We both know this. But I can't stop my past coming up."

"You can't stop yourself gathering cards and numbers now, either."

"That's not fair." I'm aware we look like two lovers having a moment right now, but inside the heat that flared has died back to embers and the hard on that threatened has retreated. "I didn't ask for the number. I talked to her because she talked to me. End of story."

"And you're going to tell me if you didn't have this whole thing you need to prove you wouldn't fucking her right now?"

"One, I'm not superman. I don't move that fast." I have, but I keep it to myself. "And two, no. I wouldn't have. I'm with you."

"You wouldn't be if you hadn't hired me."

"Fine," I say. "I wouldn't be with you if I didn't need to show I'm responsible and all the rest, but would I go home with her? Fuck no. She was hot, I won't lie, but I wasn't trying to pick her up. I was trying to get out of it."

"Out of picking her up?"

"Don't put words in my mouth, Perry. No, I was trying to get out of the flirtation. She came on like cheap perfume. Way too strong and clingy. Not my style."

"You like class now?"

I stick my face close to hers, so our lips almost touch. "I thought I did. After all, I like you."

She moves, not letting me go, but her head comes down and she places her forehead against my chest.

"Crap. You drive me crazy, Ryder. Why the hell do you get under my skin like this?"

"You were jealous." I don't know why I push that, but I like it when she sparks and spits fire. She's magnificent that way.

She's magnificent a lot of ways, but the fire stokes mine and yeah, I'm doubting I can change. Because I want her. Right or wrong, right now I want her.

Elliot lifts her head and looks at me. "I'm not jealous."

But her cheeks darken and a flush whispers up her throat and I'm fascinated. I'm calling her jealous to get a rise, but what if she actually is?

Oh, yeah, definitely turned on. Shit. I'm a terrible person. Because I want to keep poking until she loses control.

Elliot winds her hands up around my neck then. "Part of this is you knowing how to handle yourself in public, of making situations work for you."

"What—"

"So this time, I'll do it for you. We have a story to sell here, let's sell it."

"What are we going to do? Have sex here and now?"

"No, Ryder. As thrilling as that sounds, not to mention hot—"

"Sarcasm."

"—that's a definite no. So, call a car and take us to your place."

"You live right here."

She smiles and toys with a button on my shirt. "True. But we're going to your place so I can seduce you."

Chapter Eighteen

ELLIOT

The shock and dumbfounded expression on his face is laughable, or would be, if it was funny. But it isn't. Because we have a problem.

"What?" He frowns. "Seduce? *What*?"

"Is that the way to speak to your fiancée?" I can't believe I just said that. People are around us and his hands are still on me

"You just accused me of hitting on another woman."

"And you told me," I say, drawing him even closer, so close the only thing separating us are clothes and I'm pretty sure that he might be getting turned on, "that she hit on you. So, considering we're engaged—which telling me without a ring is pretty shitty and something to be rectified soon—why don't you get that car?"

I've never seen Ryder move so fast in getting a car. It's not smooth. But it's flattering. And there's that stupid part of me that wants to sink into the flattery. I won't let it, because this isn't real.

Me doing this isn't real, either. Ryder didn't see what I saw right at the end of our exchange, someone come up with their phone. So…a little show.

I'm not really into these shows, especially when I'm involved, but needs and all that. And it makes sense if we're supposedly together, then after that we'd head home.

The car's here in record time and we head to his place.

Ryder's staring at me. "You were joking."

"Was I?" Okay, I might be enjoying this a little. Having the great Ryder Sinclair off-kilter is fun. "We can just pretend I'm a woman you like, so try hard, and then you can rebuff me."

"At my place. With no one around."

"Yes."

He starts to smile. "Okay."

"There was some guy with a phone right at the end. I wanted to make it believable."

He nods, but the smile's still there. "Is that why you said we should go to my place?"

"Yes, Ryder." I breathe out heavily. "And there's a problem."

"My scandalous ways?"

"This," I say, "isn't a joke."

"Fine."

I point at him. "We need to deal with the problem at hand. How you handle yourself in public. You need a strategy."

"To repel women?"

With a nod, I say, "That's the gist."

"A strategy?" His gaze moves over me. "You're gonna help? Role play? You'll hit on me and then I'll rebuff you?"

"If I have to. And unfortunately, you need the practice at rebuffing women."

"Oh," he says, leaning back in his seat, "I do."

The car pulls up right then because let's face it, Ryder doesn't live too far from me. I know the car's overkill, but it seemed a Ryder thing to do. And it's all about the micro advancement of so-called change.

"Come on, my red-haired queen," he says, taking my hand and sweeping us out of the car and up to his door. "I'm suddenly really into homework."

I shoot him an uneasy look. He likes this a little too much.

Inside his place, we head up to the second floor and he leads me into a room I haven't been in—admittedly, the brief periods of time have been in a guest room located the floor up, and the wide living area there.

This room is different. It's industrial, but it breathes an unexpected side of Ryder I haven't seen. There is a collection of paintings on the walls. A mishmash of huge modern pieces and portraits and cityscapes, and smaller pieces. The sofas are fat and brass and black leather. There's a rug over the dark stained floor boards I know cost a fortune.

A big fireplace with neat stacks of logs lies in the center and there are guitars. Even a piano.

"The logs are for show in case you're wondering. It's an eco-fireplace."

"A fancy heater?"

"Yes." He strips off his jacket and waistcoat, down to his shirt, and rolls up the sleeves, the tattoo winding down one strong forearm. Then he unbuttons the top three and I almost salivate at the sight of smooth, golden flesh. He goes to the wet bar and pours two drinks, then holds one out to me.

I take it. "So it's just for show?" My gaze touches on the instruments, but I don't say a thing about them and neither does he.

"I told you, I like beautiful things, Elliot. But no, it's not just for show. It's a great way to heat and look good and have low environmental impact. It's a new system I put into a lot of my places I buy and sell and," he says, lifting his glass of amber liquid to his mouth and taking a sip, "if you want an in detail discussion on how it all works, you're shit out of luck. I do this crap all the time and couldn't be bothered. Besides, I'm much more interested in this rebuffing thing."

I'm standing close to him and while the heat's not on, a warmth spreads through me that's entirely to do with him.

"Fine," I mutter, taking another sip of the whiskey, into which he's added some kind of fruity syrup. It shouldn't taste good, but it does. It's like a sultry summer night on my tongue. "You're hot. Let's go home and have sex."

Ryder approaches me and looks me up and down, then shakes his head. "Nope. As sexy as that was, and believe me, it was smoking, I think you might need to try harder."

"I hate you."

"No," he says, coming in and unpinning my hair, "you don't."

"I don't do this sort of thing."

"That's not working either."

I jerk my chin at him. "I wasn't trying, I was explaining."

"Just, you know, put some feeling into it." He moves around behind me, so close I can feel the heat of him, the slight buzz of electrical awareness flare, and I'm a throb of need deep down inside. "Say it like you mean it."

I close my eyes. This was my stupid idea. Gulping down half the drink, I spin to face him. "Hey there, big boy, you're looking mighty fine. How about it?"

A slow smile spreads and I know he's having the time of his life. "How about what?"

"You know…"

"Chess? You want to play chess with me?"

"You're an asshole."

"And you're not trying." He takes my glass and sets it down on the bar with his. "Why don't you say, 'fuck you're one sexy man, Ryder Sinclair. How about we get naked and do the deed?'"

"I'm not saying that."

He nods, slips a hand around my waist and pulls me in and weak creature I am, I let him. "Fair enough. What about…I've been lost in the desert for weeks and you're the oasis I need to survive?"

"Or how about do me now or I kill you?"

"I like your style, Perry," he murmurs, the fingers of his free hands smoothing down over my hair, then winding the ends about them. "Sexy and scary and strong."

"I don't do this, Ryder."

"Don't do what?"

"I don't go around propositioning men."

His mouth skims against my ear. "Neither do I. Seems we're both on a learning curve."

"Focus, Ryder."

"Oh, believe me, I'm focused."

His words, that subtle thread running through them, wind about me and threaten to steal the air from my lungs. "How are you going to rebuff someone?"

"Thing is," he says, "I don't. Not usually."

I go to pull away so I can gather my thoughts, but his hand tightens at my waist.

"What I mean is I tend to see someone I like. They see me, and they get the message. They send the message. Otherwise, I just don't."

My gaze darts to him. "Your ego knows no bounds."

"Maybe, but it's the truth. Other times, it's just talk and one thing leads to another."

"So you'd have slept with her?"

He's silent. Then he says, "No. I'd have talked, found a way out, probably gotten a number I'd never use, and that would be that." Those dark eyes search mine. "I was distracted."

This man should never be allowed out alone. He looks at me like there's no one else on the planet worth his time and no wonder that blonde went for me. No female wants to lose that to another.

"Trying to be good?"

"By you."

Ryder lets go of my hair and slides his palm against my face and he kisses me. It's a different kiss to the others. This kiss is deliberately slow, and the onslaught is deadly and delicious, and I can't stop myself from kissing him back. My mouth opens to his and he takes that offer and runs.

The kiss is pure heat and fantasy, it's wet and hot and night. It's seduction at its finest and I'm helpless against it.

I know all the reasons I shouldn't. But I can't stop myself. I wind around him, making a noise in the back of my throat, one that gets a response from him. And it's not until it's like we're flying down I realize he's got us sprawled on one of the sofas. The kisses are a hot, dark onslaught now. And he moves down my throat to bite and suck at my jugular, and then back up to claim my mouth.

And I'm helpless to anything but respond. I'm his. In that moment, I'm his.

I want everything there is.

His hands move over me, touching and caressing and I'm just holding on, a mess of need and throbbing pleasure. Everything in me is alive.

On fire.

He slides his hand up my thigh, then up along my hip, and he's touching the bare flesh of my torso. It flutters beneath that attention. And his fingers move higher, beneath my shirt, to the lace of my bra and then he's inside it, his touch magic and I almost come from that.

When his fingers catch my nipple, I'm not lost. I'm surrendering.

Whatever happens next, I'm his.

Chapter Nineteen

RYDER

Elliot is the most exquisite thing. She's gorgeous. I see that now. The passion on her face, the need, the way her body moves against mine. The way she kisses. The way she feels. Her mind. All of it comes together like some kind of supernova of enlightenment and she's completely gorgeous.

And I'm about to fuck her.

I drag a deep breath in to my lungs and I stop, burying my head in her shoulder as I struggle to get myself under control.

She's still. My hand is on her breast, beneath her shirt and bra, and I'm so hard it's a wonder I don't come.

I meant...I don't know what I meant. But she didn't want this.

She wanted it. On that physical level and I know how to play a woman.

She wants it, but she also doesn't want it. I know that.

It's that simple and that complicated.

"I'm rebuffing you." The words sound ludicrous the moment I say them, muffled though they are.

Elliot shoves at me and then pushes until I let myself tumble to the ground. There, I lean my back against the sofa and try to restore my breathing and my body to pre seduction mode. To pre losing control mode.

Because yeah, I lost control.

"You're rebuffing me."

"Yes." I push the word out. "That's what we're doing, right? Playing a game?"

And as I say that, I don't want this to be a game. I'm not sure what it is I want it to be, other than real. Something that's going to happen because we both want each other. Want each other beyond a stupid game. Beyond the roles we have. Beyond the stakes and the job I hired her to do.

Holy fuck. I like her.

That's why I took it too far. I like her.

The knowledge sinks down into the marrow of my bones.

And I don't know what to do with it. She's meant to be my friend and I've crossed a line and into a lust situation. I like her, I'm attracted to her and how the fuck do I say that without sounding like, well, Ryder Sinclair? The guy who doesn't date, who doesn't have relationships, how does he tell a woman he's found he likes that he likes her as in not just friendship?

I'm like some kind of awkward fucking kid.

She thinks I'm a horn dog, a fuck boy. She's told me I'm a fuck boy. She's called me a man whore. And...she's not wrong. I still don't see anything wrong with that because it's who and what I am and I don't judge anyone else on that. But I like her.

Liking and wanting something beyond fucking her are different worlds. I don't know what I want in that regard. Beyond the sex. If I want anything.

"Were we?"

There's a note in her voice that makes bells ring inside in the distance. Not good bells, either. But what is it she wants?

We're different people. Hardwired in completely incompatible ways. I'm betting Elliot's never had a one-night stand. Never gone out on the town to find someone just to fuck and forget.

I've never gone looking for a picket fence. Or even a rental with someone.

Again, I don't know what to do with any of that.

Seems like the great fucking Ryder Sinclair doesn't know anything at all except that he wants to fuck the redhead in the room, who wants to see if her tits fit his hands perfectly once more.

"Wasn't that the point of all this?"

She kicks me. Not hard, it's more a shove and I don't blame her. I'm being a bastard.

"No, Ryder. You weren't supposed to teach me a lesson. That's cruel."

"I'm not being cruel, Elliot. I'm not a cruel person. You can think of me what you want, think I'm worth nothing, but I'm never cruel to someone." I stop, get to my feet and pour myself a whiskey neat, down it and do it again. Setting the glass down, I grip the edge of the wet bar. "At least, not deliberately."

"Why did you kiss me?"

"Because..." Shit. She might be attracted to me. I'm not an idiot. And there's chemistry. I'm never an idiot about that. But Elliot's made it clear what she thinks of me, and she sees me as a failure in some fundamental way. "You were there."

"I was there? That's the answer? The other kisses, they happened because others were there, but Ryder, you crossed a line here."

"Of course I did. Isn't that me all over? Isn't that why I hired you? Because I'm the fuck up who won't stop giving?"

Something lands next to the bar and I look down and shake my head. "I'm not sure what I'm more astounded by...the fact you threw a shoe at me or you own Jimmy Choos."

"I can't have pretty things?"

"You can and you should," I say, turning to face her.

Her eyes are too big. They're vulnerable and her clothes are disheveled, along with her hair. She looks glorious. She also holds her other shoe in her hands like she wants to aim it at my head this time.

"Do you take anything seriously? I thought you wanted this."

"If you're going to throw the shoe, try to hit me and not anything else. Some of this stuff's expensive," I say.

She looks at the shoe and then at me. "Everything in this place has a hefty price tag, but I think the problem is, Ryder, you don't know the worth of anything."

"Bullshit."

"You tell me you want the Sinclair jewels because of your family history and they mean something. You tell me you don't want to lose the family flagship company for the same reasons, yet here you are, fucking about."

She makes sense. She really does. But she's utterly and spectacularly wrong. I take a step towards her. "First off, things in here are a mix. But just like the jewels and the company, I want them because they mean something. To me. I'm not an art collector. I got these pieces because I like them. Some of them remind me of places I went. Some of them are because of the artist. I don't need to surround myself with hefty price tags to show the world I can afford them. I don't give a fuck about what the world thinks. I don't invite the world here. And what I told you about why I'm doing this is the truth."

"Then stop fucking around."

But," I say, "there's another truth with that. I don't want the loss to be on my shoulders. I know that's selfish, but hey, you knew that."

She shakes her head and looks at the shoe again. "Then clean up your act, Ryder. Most people can keep it in their pants, can keep scandal at bay for a few weeks. For a few months. You're not trying to get famous, you want something and yet you keep screwing up."

"I kissed you."

Color, deep red, flares in her cheeks and something in me twists. "Don't."

"Don't kiss you."

"Jesus, Ryder. You're not that hard up."

I frown. "What's hard up with kissing you?"

"We don't have an audience, so you don't need to go there. We were meant to be practicing you handling yourself on the public stage, and if that's really how you do it, then we really have a major problem."

I shove a hand through my hair and stalk up to her. "I don't go around just kissing people, Elliot. I kissed you. And..." I trail off. Fuck, I'm going to have to tell her. "I did it because I wanted to."

"Great," she says, spitting the word, "you get bored and let some stupid urge take you over because I'm the only female in the room."

"Is that so bad?"

She stares at me like I've grown fangs and it hits me how that sounded, I go to say something, to explain, but she shakes her head. "Don't dig your hole deeper, Ryder, otherwise you won't be able to get out. And yes, it is bad. What woman, even one like me, wants to hear that?"

Frustration swells inside, tightening my throat and chest and I clench my hands because damn I want to grab her and I'm not sure if it's to kiss or shake sense into her. Or if it's just because I want to touch her. "A woman like you? One who thinks I'm beneath her?"

"No." The scathing burns like acid. "What was the word you used? Oh, yes, frump."

"You can't be serious, Perry. I used that about your work clothes, not you."

"So?"

"So...? You're pretty, you should shine, I told you that."

She turns from me, then swings back. "If this is you trying another rebuff then you suck at it. You need to be smooth with it, not try and jump someone and then awkwardly get out of it."

"You're the most deliberately obtuse and stubborn woman I know. I wasn't rebuffing you then."

"Good, because you suck at it."

"Suck at what? Rebuffing? I haven't really tried."

Elliot pushes past me for her glass and takes it. I pluck it out of her hands and finish it because she's pissing me off.

"Give me that." She snatches it and grabs the whiskey and sloshes it into the glass, then she takes a huge swallow, turns red and coughs. "Oh, that burns."

"Like you."

"I don't burn." She takes another swallow, this one smaller. "I don't even know what that means."

"It means you're a pain in my ass." I stare at her. "This isn't about rebuffing, is it? This is about you being all butt hurt and I don't know why."

"That's your problem. You take for yourself and never bother to understand anyone else and their needs."

"What needs are you on about? You were trying to get me to rebuff you and you looked good and I...I kissed you."

She jabs a finger at me. "See? You just took for yourself."

"No, you idiot. Okay, yes, but that wasn't the reasoning. I don't go about thinking oh, I'll just take this. I did it because I like you. I wanted to kiss you because I'm attracted to you."

Silence falls and we both look at each other. Her shock is insulting, but not really surprising to me.

"I didn't mean to say it just like that." It had been gauche and not me. But this is new for me. I'm all sucker punched and I don't know why.

And Elliot looks for all the world like she's like waiting for the floor to swallow her whole.

This might be one of the lowest points in my life. I'm being rejected by Elliot.

"We're friends, I know that," I say. "I don't want to lose that, but I can't help liking you, too."

"Don't lie to me, Ryder."

"I'm not."

"You? You like me?"

"Yes." I move in a little closer. "It might not be what you want, but..."

She laughs. She actually laughs and shakes her head and it dawns on me that she might like me, too. At least on some level.

"But," I say, "it is what it is."

"What it is, is you being bored."

"No." Now I take hold of her and draw her close, right up against me, and she makes a little hiss of sound that slides down to my cock. "What it is, is me liking you, wanting you. I'll show you."

And I kiss her again.

A soft, sweet kiss.

"You think," she says, "you can just kiss me and I'll melt?"

"Oh, Elliot, I know that."

It's the one thing I know. It's a skill and fuck it all. I'm going to use it.

This time I kiss her slow and long and I take my time, I bite soft on her lower lips, draw it into my mouth and run my tongue over that sensitive flesh, and then I delve in, a deliberate dance of seduction, and exploration designed to draw her out, to dissolve her.

She's kissing me back now. And it's easy, so easy, to slide down into her, to just give over to the passion building.

I lift my head.

"Want me to show you more?"

She's dazed. And I have her where I want her. I'm back on familiar ground.

So I go in for the kill.

Chapter Twenty

ELLIOT

If I thought I was lost before, I wasn't. I'm lost now. And I'm a willing participant in that.

Ryder's a powerhouse of passion and magnetism and not only am I helpless, I want to be.

I want what's on offer.

I want him.

I might hate him. Because in the eroticism of the kiss what he said comes back to me and I pull away, gasping for breath, for something to hold on to, a tiny piece of common sense that will keep me anchored and away from letting myself fall completely into him and the insanity and heat of doing that.

"Ryder, you don't have to keep this up," I say. "You know the effect you have on women."

"It's you, Elliot." He kisses my ear, drawing my lobe into his mouth and sucking on it, sending a throbbing beat of pleasure straight down to my clit. He lets go and his lips brush my ear as he speaks in a low, dark tone that's full of sex and promises. "Not women. You. And right here and now I want you."

I know those words are a warning. The right here and now part. They're not a forever, they're not even a future or another night after this. He's talking about just for now. That's all it is.

And I can see it, what he does, how women fall for him.

He tells them the truth and they go willingly, open-eyed, open-armed, open-legged. Because they can see he's promising them a slice of something spectacular, something to take to the grave, to remember on cold and lonely nights.

And it's why none of them hate him. He gives them nothing but right here and now, and they snap it up and for all I want to see myself as someone different, I'm not.

I want that shining, exquisite moment, too.

"Ryder..."

He's touching me again, his hands sliding under my shirt, over my back, and his mouth is kissing a heated, delicious trail down my throat. He bites. Hard enough to make me moan and clutch at him, to make my clit send a wave of pleasure undulating through me.

Holy shit. He just made me come.

It was a flutter of an orgasm, but it was there and oh, yeah, I want.

"You're a bastard," I say, taking hold of his head and kissing him hard. "You're doing this deliberately."

"Yeah, I am. I want you, Perry. I want every single part of you. I want to make you scream. I want to watch you when you come. And I mean come for real."

"Asshole."

I bite his lip, hard, and he groans, his fingers digging into my flesh as he moves me backwards across the room. His dark eyes glitter with need and lust. Not triumph. Just like his world begins and ends with me and him and heat and sex.

He bites back, harder. And another throb of need and pleasure rolls through me. "I can tell when a woman comes. I can make you come. I can control when you do, too. And right then, you almost did, not like the small one you had before. That was just a taste, Elliot."

The light changes and we're in the hall. He kisses me then. Dark and deep and full of erotic hunger and everything in me is focused on that.

He pulls one hand away and hits something on the wall, and then we're moving again, and I'm too busy kissing him back, my hands buried in his hair, to think about where we are until something dings and then we're moving again.

An elevator. Of course he has an elevator.

I need him. And he's acting like he needs me too.

We keep kissing and touching, the heat growing along with the hunger and need.

Ryder spins me and I hit a wall and he's there, mouth on me, hands under my ass, lifting me and I go willingly, melting up into him as he lifts me and there's a moment of real shock, as my pussy is suddenly rubbing against his cock.

We're clothed, there's too much material in the way, but he's hard and hot and oh, God, big.

Ryder lifts his mouth from mine. "I really want to fuck you, Elliot."

"Good. Because I need you to fuck me."

He takes my mouth, ravishes me, and I return that onslaught with one of my own. "I want to do this right." He sets me down and we're at each other, pulling at each other's clothes. Buttons fly along with items of clothes until we're naked. His gaze rakes over me. A long, slow exploration that makes me feel like a queen, like I'm glorious, like I'm special.

"You're incredible," he says.

His fingers brush against my nipples and I take him in, too. I don't think I've ever seen a man hotter than him, more beautiful. It's everything about him. His cock, proud and erect and thick, those muscular long legs, those washboard abs. Did I mention his cock?

I wrap my fingers around him and I start to jerk him off. Long, low, deliberate movements, brushing my thumb over the precum at the head, squeezing.

He grabs my hand and holds it there. "You keep that up and you're not going to get this job done to your satisfaction."

"You telling me the great Ryder Sinclair might perform a little early?"

He lifts my hand away and kisses my palm. "The way you do that? Definitely."

And he kisses me again, wrapping about me and he takes me down to the bed, turning us so one of his thighs is between mine.

This time his mouth moves slow and deep on mine. The kisses are drugging, drawing me into him and he explores me, leaving a trail of glittering fire wherever he touches, down and down, until he reached the apex of my thighs.

There he slides his fingers along me, along my pussy, through the wetness, teasing me. And I push down, seeking more. Ryder laughs softly and he parts my pussy lips and thrusts two fingers into me, making me cry out at the sweet, wanted invasion. I'm tingling and throbbing and the kiss turns fierce as he curls his fingers up and starts working both my g-spot and my clit at the same time.

He breaks the kiss, making his way down my body, burning a path with his mouth until he's there, between my thighs, and, with his fingers still working me, he licks my clit, drawing it into his mouth and suckling and I cry out at the intense wave that crashes over me.

I rush forward into that pleasure. It's a sprint to the top, and I come, exploding. And I'm clawing at him, wriggling my hips and dragging my clit from him and moaning, crying, saying words that don't make sense and Ryder doesn't stop.

Instead, he moves back up, kissing my lips, then slides down again, kissing a trail from my lips down my throat, taking his time, and I try and push him away because I'm shuddering, I'm so sensitive, but he won't stop. He keeps up the rhythm.

And as he does so, the pressure and pleasure starts to build again and he works me harder, this time adding small bites and licks as he kisses that path down to my breasts. He takes my nipple in his mouth and he sucks hard, bringing his teeth down on it and I scream.

I come again. Harder, more violently than the last time.

And Ryder stops, pulling his hand free.

He lines himself up and lifts his head, looking down into my eyes as he thrusts into me.

I'm a mess of want and need and everything is too much and not enough and I wrap about him as he starts to thrust into me, slow and steady, long strokes that go so deep I gasp every time.

Still, he watches me as he does so. And he keeps that pace and I'm spiraling up again. I can't believe it, but I am. I'm on the edge and Ryder knows. "Come for me again," he whispers.

"I...can't..."

"Yeah, you can. Come, Elliot. Give yourself to me."

And incredibly, I start to shake apart again, my body convulsing around him and I can't see, and he's there, his mouth on mine and then his control dissolves and he's kissing me hard and fast, pounding into me and I'm kissing him back, raising my hips to meet him.

There's so much pressure inside, like it's way too much, like he needs to stop, but then it morphs into something else. Something so deep and wild that I'm swept up in him.

"Harder, Ryder. Fuck. Harder. More."

He obliges and this isn't a masterful onslaught. This is raw, unadulterated need. And there's nothing but him and me and we're rutting, fucking, going at each other so hard that it's like we want to be in the other. It's wild. Animalistic. Heat and need so intense there's nothing else but him and me and I want more.

And then he comes, setting me off. And we fly.

I'm satiated, limp, like a boneless creature adrift on a sea of sweet languid warmth when we're done.

We stay like that, joined, for a long moment or ten after, both of us sweat slicked, breathing hard. His weight is on me and it's good. But all things end, I guess, and after that eternity, that moment, he kisses me and sighs.

He pulls out and I think Ryder's going to move away, leave the room, I don't know. I think he's going to do something, anything except what he does do. Ryder pulls me into his embrace and curls around me, holding me close, his mouth on my forehead, even though we're both slick with sweat and sex.

I don't know how much time passes, but I know I can't regret it. How could I?

I've never ever had that before. Not something so erotic and intense and beautiful and raw. It's a moment out of time. It's this night and nothing more and I can't find it in me to regret having a taste of Ryder Sinclair.

If it's like that for him always, then no wonder he's the way he is. And no wonder women drop their clothes like they're taking a breath when it comes to being asked into his bed.

He's smoothing his fingers over my hair and it's a loving move, or it feels loving, even though I know it isn't.

Ryder likes me. He says we're friends. And I honestly don't know if I can go back to that place we were at before this. Not when the job is done and dusted. If he wanted to keep being friends.

Yes, he's attracted to me. But I know that's Ryder. He's attracted to women.

"You okay, Elliot?"

The soft tenderness in his tone makes my eyes prickle and I rub my head against him, reveling in the touch, the feel, the heat, the smell of him.

"Of course."

"That was...fuck. That was insane," he says. "You blow my mind, Perry."

"It's me, Ryder, you don't need to say these things."

"I know that." He brushes his lips over my hair. "But I want to."

"Crap."

He shifts, and his fingers slide beneath my chin and he lifts my face to his so we're looking at each other. "Regrets?"

"Not right now. No."

"Good." A soft smile plays over that beautiful mouth. "Me either."

"I don't think you regret anything."

He laughs. "There are regrets, everyone has them. But not over this. Not about you and me."

"Ryder..."

"We should talk—"

"No." I lift my hand to his lips and place it there. "We shouldn't."

The smile and laughter vanish. "Why not?"

"Because isn't that enough? I see it now. Why women want you beyond that face. But this is just you and me and now."

"Come on, Elliot. This is different."

"How is it different? Don't ruin this."

I push him down onto his back and straddle him and he begins to stir again. I decide to help him along by stroking my fingers over him, and he grows under my touch.

It's a powerful thing, knowing I can do that.

"Fuck, Elliot. That isn't fair. It's hard to think straight when you have your hand on me."

"Oh, poor Ryder. Whatever shall we do?"

His eyes narrow, but the smile appears again. "I have a lot of ideas. But I think you should stop and we should talk."

"No, we shouldn't. Don't ruin this, Ryder. I think we should just get this out of our systems. Tonight is a night out of time."

"Elliot—"

I kiss him hard and then I lift myself and tease the head of his cock with my pussy and he hisses a breath. "Let's just get this out of our systems."

"You want more?"

"What can I say? You've opened a voracious beast in me. She's here for one night only."

"I can do more."

"So stop talking."

And I sink down on him. Right down until he's completely in me. I'm so full, I'm already beginning to tingle. I start to rock my hips.

"I think I can do that." And Ryder lets me take him.

I move, kissing him, rocking my body over him, moving harder and faster, adjusting to get him hitting that place in me just right and soon we're both lost and we come.

It's not the end for the night. No, because the lightness and the conversation melt until it's just us. And the intensity sweeps us and we keep coming back to each other like we can't get enough.

And we do it over and over again.

Chapter Twenty-One

RYDER

I don't know when I pass out. But when I wake, it's quiet and the bed is empty.

That's fine. Great. It's how I like it. No complications. No one needs to know and my asshole family can keep having their side bets and no one needs to know about this...this...this glitch.

No one at all.

Of course there's me. And the lovely Elliot. We know. And we'll have to deal with it.

Knowing her, she's going to pretend it didn't happen.

I'm home free.

I lie back for about two seconds before I'm up and yanking on my clothes, shoving my feet in sneakers and out the door.

It's quiet, cold at almost five a.m. in TriBeCa and I march the streets, cutting off cars as I cross the roads until I'm at her building.

I ring the damn buzzer, pressing down again and again until she answers.

"Let me in, Perry, or I'm going to cause such a scene you won't be able to appear on the streets of this damn fucking city for a week."

She buzzes me in.

When I reach her apartment, I storm past her into her space and slam the door. Then I glare. "What the actual fuck?"

"I went home, Ryder. Why are you here?" She crosses her arms and glares back. "And I should have let you cause that scene you so charmingly threatened. You'd lose your little dream."

"So?" Right then I don't care. "It would be worth it to piss you off."

"I don't see why you're so angry. I just took the awkwardness out of it. Of course, until you turned up here, bringing it with you. Are you the only one allowed to bow out, that it?"

I point a finger at her. Because I am angry. I'm furious. It bubbles up, lava hot and I don't know if she's right or wrong here, only that I didn't want her to leave.

More. I wanted more. Want more.

I point a finger at her and say, "You wouldn't let me do that."

"That's your response, is it? I wouldn't let you ruin the effort I've put into trying to make you a decent human?"

"Decent?"

Okay, so I hadn't meant to say that to her, but what am I meant to say? I didn't want her to go? I stare at my finger, at her, and then I breathe out and push my hair back from her face. "What are you wearing?"

"Things to sleep in, Ryder." She waves a hand over the T-shirt and the boy shorts that show her long, shapely legs off.

"You usually wear ugly pajamas."

"My apartment's warm tonight and—" She stops and comes up to me and pokes me in the chest hard. "You're a total ass, Ryder. You don't know how to talk to women beyond seduction and sex."

"That's a lie." The words come out a little uncertain.

"You know it's not. Think about it. We had a moment and that was fine and now you're back to judging what I'm wearing and being...actually, I don't know what you're being. It's not abandoned. Because you don't get abandoned. You usually do that. I just went home. I figured you'd be happy about that and we could move on."

Something dark and cold moves through me. "Is that what it was? A moment?"

"Yes. Wasn't it?"

I don't know what to say. We have two areas. The uncharted waters that state There Be Dragons for me, waters I never wade into. Or we have the safe and familiar, the what it is, just move on and pretend it didn't happen. She seems great at that. I should be even better. I'm not sure I am.

Because Elliot's different from everyone and anyone I've met.

"It was a moment," she says, voice flat. "And it was done, so I left."

"You can't leave."

"I did."

"I mean, you can't walk out on me. I need you there. By my side. I'm paying you."

Everything in her face shuts down. She's a wall of spiked brick. And I immediately know it was the wrong thing to say. I want to pull her into my arms and seduce her. I want to taste those lips, have all that warm, soft flesh pressed against me. I want to drop to my knees and explore her sweet, hot pussy with my mouth.

I want a lot of things that her stony, barbed expression says I'm not getting.

"Elliot—"

"Go home, Ryder. I'm taking the problematic element out of this thing. We had sex. That's it. We don't talk about it. We pretend it didn't happen. You get the best of all the worlds. Sex with no complications, and that should hopefully be enough to tide you over, because it's not happening again."

"You don't know that."

"A repeat performance? No."

"Elliot, you're twisting this, I want—"

"I know what you want. You got it. We get through this by forgetting tonight. We get through this by you doing what I say. Now, there's an opening of an arts foundation that does a lot of charity work coming up. You're going, it's the kind of thing up the alley of the Sinclair board. Keep it in your pants, and try not to fuck someone on your way home." She marches past me, opening her door.

We look at each other and I'm not done. Her body, her face, every charged ion in the air says she is.

"Goodbye, Ryder."

I start to say something but think better of it, and head back out into the very early morning without a backward glance.

After all, she's gone and saved me the trouble of getting out of whatever this is at a later date.

And I tell myself that's a good thing. A very good thing, indeed.

"I'm not in a fucking mood," I say, glaring at Kingston, who's currently haunting my Park Avenue office.

He stares out the window at the bright afternoon, then turns back to me, sliding his hands in his trouser pockets. "You never could lie for shit, Ry," he says. "I've a mind to up the stakes and take it all. You slept with her."

"When has anyone in this family become so obsessed with my sex life?"

He shrugs and grins and comes over to the seat opposite my large wood and steel desk, a sleek thing that's a masterpiece in modern design. "Since you stopped really having one."

"So has the side bet become the top bet?"

"Not really, but I could make it that. You know I don't care about tricking the others out of their money."

My phone buzzes but I ignore it. I know who it is. And that I haven't seen her in a few days annoys the hell out of me. It annoys the hell out of me even more that I'm annoyed.

"You're fucking loaded, like the rest of us, you dick. Why do you want money that means nothing?"

"Money always means something," he says, reasonably. "Small or large amounts. It adds up." Then King pins me with a hard look. "When's the next board meeting?"

"I'd prefer it if you were all there."

"Our father had a sense of humor." He puts his feet on my desk and I send him an irritated look, one he ignores. "Who knew?"

"I'm not sure it's a sign of a sense of humor to fuck with your kids after you're gone. And you three are on the board, so…"

"Stipulations. We're not invited. They want to see you handle yourself without our guidance. Pity the old man never cottoned on to the fact we have no say over what the fuck you do or how you do it."

Yeah. Our heritage in my hands. "So you care?"

"The company is worth a fortune, and also a fortune beyond money on paper. It if goes public, then who the hell knows who'll get their grubby hands on a piece. Plus, it makes us look weak and that's across everything."

I nod slowly and slump back in my seat. "Just because I like sex, women, and a good time, I have to become a conservative asshat to show I can do what I already do."

"As I said, sense of fucking humor."

"Jesus." I get up and start to pace, and my phone buzzes on my desk again. "No one has faith in me."

"We do and you know it. It's not about that. It's about a game. And I really wouldn't give a flying fuck if we weren't dragged into this with the family business being dangled as some kind of bait. Shit, I'd let the jewels go—my piece—if I didn't think they're worth a fortune. They're already the stuff of legend and lore, imagine if we had them all together on display, and sold them to the highest bidder."

I wince. "You have no soul, and no one else will do that."

"So, I'll sell mine." My phone buzzes again. "Aren't you going to get that?"

"Nope."

"I knew you fucked your make over artist."

Heat rises along the back of my neck. "Elliot isn't a make over artist. And it's none of your business."

"Is that all?" I add, suddenly done with the conversation. "I've got an event to go to."

"That thing tonight? I'll see you there." He gets up and heads to the door. "And your Elliot."

"Not my anything!"

He's lucky I like my shoes enough I don't launch them at his smug head as he disappears.

Elliot's waiting for me when I get home. She follows me in without a word and I dump my coat on the sofa and deposit myself next to it. "I can do this myself, you know."

"No," she says, "you can't. That's why you hired me."

Shit. I know she's right and that's not what my problem is. My problem is her.

She's acting like nothing happened between us and for some reason I can't do that thing I do, which is just go on like it didn't happen. Or go on like it happened and nothing changed.

It happened.

Everything changed.

I'm not sure how, because I've had hot sex before. I've had times where I've lost track of the time I've spent with a woman. But for some reason, Elliot is different. I want her to acknowledge the buzz in the air, the awareness that flares bright and hot between us. I want her to say her world changed, too.

I want to do it again.

"Elliot, listen."

Her flick of a gaze is a warning. "I'm not sure I can make it tonight, so I figured we'd go—"

"Why? Because of the other night?"

A blush blooms on her face. "No. I just don't know if I can."

"It happened. Call it a moment, pretend it didn't happen, but it did." I get to my feet. "And this thing isn't part time. I'm paying you a lot of money to be there."

"Ryder, I'm not your slave."

"I know that." How the fuck do I keep getting things wrong when it comes to her? Anyone else and they'd be eating out of my hand. I open my mouth with her and all the wrong things come out when all I want to do is make things better.

Maybe I've been body snatched.

"What I'm trying to say is I need you." I approach her, but I don't touch. I get the feeling she won't welcome that right now. "I need you, and I want you, Elliot. I want you there with me."

"Ryder..."

"I want you with me because outside all of this, outside of the job I hired you for, I think you're good for me, and I like you. And you're also way prettier than you think."

Those last words are inspired because yes, I mean them, but she seems to believe she's plain and no one sees her. But I do, and I want her to know that. I want—

"Gee," she says in a voice dripping with sarcasm. "Thanks, Ryder. Now that you, God of Beauty, have spoken, I'll go to the ball. Sing songs. Believe in myself."

"You know what I meant."

She sighs. "Yes, I think I do, and I also think you need to pack up your shovel and put it away before you get into all kinds of horrible trouble with that hole you're digging."

Elliot has a point. I'm not being inspired. I'm being an idiot. I'm mangling an already mangled situation.

"Okay," I say, "so you might not be coming tonight." I nod. "Let's focus on the plan..."

The event is as boring and staid as I thought. My brothers are there, and Kingston studies me, but doesn't say a word.

"Shut up, King."

He only smiles. That expression tells me way too many things I don't want to hear. Like the mighty are falling, and where's Elliot.

She's not here. And I move past my brothers to the bar, making small talk along the way. My mother is also there, but I ignore her, too. I'm not in the mood for anything other than meaningless small talk.

"Hello," says a beautiful woman with short black hair. She trails a hand over my suit, tucking something into my pocket. "Call me."

I'm on my best behavior, I tell myself, watching as she sashays away with that sweet extra swing to her hips.

Sweet, but totally manufactured.

I still appreciate it. Even if it isn't the compact yet low-key sexy way Elliot moves. I get a drink. I sip the champagne, figuring that if I just keep to myself I can be on my best behavior and not get into trouble.

To help me out, I pull out my phone and scroll through work emails, which is the perfect crutch and excuse on multiple levels.

"Ryder!" Leah something or other that I slept with a few years go bumps into me and she's all smiles and secret looks. "Long time."

There's a big diamond ring glittering on her finger and I breathe out a sigh of relief. Off limits. "How are you?"

"You know." She waggles her hand at me and then smooths a hand over my lapel. "He's very nice, very rich, and I probably won't introduce you to him."

"I'm happy for you. He's a lucky guy."

She makes a small sound as she sips her champagne. "You know, it's a pity I love him or else I'd be tempted."

"I'm not offering."

Leah looks at me and curls a strand of her blonde hair behind her ear. "I'd be asking, but…that's interesting. Oh, hang on…"

She opens her small crystal encrusted clutch and pulls out a card and hands it to me. "My number. Not for that, but my cousin is looking for something wonderful in the West Village and I thought of you. If you have anything, call my work number or email. It's there."

Then she pulls me down as she goes up on her toes and kisses my cheek. "Talk to you soon, Ryder."

She leaves and I stare after her, the card still in my hand.

I'm feeling good at how I handled that. Of how it went. I didn't flirt, I made sure she knew there wasn't a chance in case that's what she was looking for and no one got hurt.

It's then that I look up.

Elliot.

I shove the card into my pocket and smile, trying to tamp down the sudden panic at having numbers I didn't ask for.

"I thought," she says, sliding in next to me at the bar, the shimmery green dress that skims her sweet body and flares to just below her knees in a swirl of material as she does so is deceptively sexy, "I should come and make sure you were still alive."

She gives me a glance over her shoulder, her red hair falling in loose waves around her as she asks for a drink.

How the fuck I ever thought her plain is beyond me. Elliot isn't. She's absolutely stunning.

She gets her drink and turns to face me. "You look good. The picture of what the board wants."

As her gaze moves over me, she frowns. And panic starts to throb deep in me. She's staring at my pocket.

I look down.

Fuck.

Right there is a cream corner of cardboard.

And without another word, she reaches over and takes it.

Not just the card from Leah, but the other one, too.

Fuck.

Chapter Twenty-Two

ELLIOT

"I can explain."

Ryder's words shoot through me. And I keep staring at the cards in my hand, willing it not to shake.

Of all the things he could have said, those three words are up there among the worst.

"You're collecting numbers, Ryder."

"No, well, I know one of the women and she wants—"

"We all know what they want. I thought we went through how to handle all this. Or are you just trying to get a jump on the time you're free? You know, like a collection plate, but with women instead of money."

He snatches the cards back. Looks at them, then shoves them at me. "No. Jesus, it would be nice, just for once, for someone to believe in me."

He can't change. I know that now. Whatever excuse he might come up with, he can't. Ryder's hard wired to want women. As in plural. One could never satisfy him. Abstinence certainly wasn't doable for him, and now, right after we have sex—or near enough—he's at it again.

"You keep this shit up, Ryder, and you're going to lose."

"I have just over two weeks left."

"And you can't help yourself."

His eyes burn dark fire. "Some chick put her card in my pocket. I know Leah. And yeah, you want to know? We did. Ages ago. She's happily engaged now. She wants me to help her cousin find a place. That's all. I let her know I wasn't interested. I might have jumped the gun, but I was trying to have it out there I wasn't interested. That I'm not available. It's why I'm standing here like an asshole. And you..."

He stops, shakes his head and signals to the bartender. "Bourbon, straight up, please." Then he glares at me. "And you brand me and damn me without a trial. I didn't do anything wrong."

I take deep, calming breaths. "This isn't the place for this discussion."

Am I being unreasonable? There's a part of me that's sure I am, because that's the part who walked out before he could do that to me, metaphorically speaking. If I set those personal rules, this can't hurt as much, right?

But there's the professional Elliot at play, here, too. And she knows he needs hard core.

Because I haven't failed in my job and I'm not about to start, not with Ryder Sinclair.

Too many people are looking at us, including his brothers. All tall, all dark, all impossibly good looking. And Ryder's the most beautiful one of them all. He could walk into a room dressed like a hobo and people would gravitate. He's beautiful and he has presence and that's part of why this thing with him is so difficult. If he blended in, it wouldn't matter. I'd be able to be more hands off. But couple his looks with his personality, his allure and his way with women, then...

Under the circumstances of the job, he's a disaster always waiting to happen.

His hand curls around mine and I almost rip it from his grip. He's too there, too real. The heat and electricity of his touch tumbles through me and pushes hard against the flimsy walls I've built.

"Don't fight, Perry."

"I'm not."

"You're about to." He murmurs this against my ear and I try not to shiver. "And my mother is avidly watching. Along with my brothers."

And half the room, even if they're pretending not to. I smile up at him, even though I don't feel it inside. "Fine. We can take this elsewhere."

"Or we can forget it."

"Not a chance, not if you want me to work for you."

He nods. "You win, for now."

And with that, we make our way outside and we wait until his car arrives. I slide in and he follows. We're silent as we drive across town, the streets of Manhattan melting past us.

We pull up in Greenwich Village outside what looks to be one of those charming residential streets just off Bank Street.

Ryder gets out and holds the door, offering me his hand which I ignore. There's a building set back amongst a small garden of trees beyond a brick wall. From inside, music tinkles out and Ryder heads up the path to the door where he flashes the woman just inside a card. She waves us in.

"Private club. Old school," he says as we wind down the hall of polished dark wood. He pushes open a door and we go into a small room with a bar and lush private booths. It's full of older, suited men, some smoking cigars, the acrid scent burning my nose.

There are young women in tight dresses draped over some of them, but most are there, deep in conversation while some classical music plays over discreet speakers.

He points to a booth and then signals the waiter and orders drinks. All this is done so fast and smoothly I know it's not his first time. This isn't a part of Manhattan I'm privy to, although I'm aware such places exist. They'd have been a gentleman's club in the classier aspect of the word back in the day and I'm assuming it's private with the cigar smoking.

"I fucking hate this place," he says as two martinis appear discreetly. "Just so you're aware. My father came here. It's a place to do deals and talk business—"

"And flaunt girls."

"Those are wives," he says, barely flickering a glance. "And I hate this kind of shit. But it's private and discreet and I didn't think you wanted to come to my place."

"Ryder."

He ignores the warning. "On account of all the hot sex we had."

"Ryder."

He takes a swig of the martini and I almost smile at the savagery. "Thing is, tonight I didn't do anything wrong and you're acting like I did."

"You had numbers."

"So?" He sounds hard and brutal as he says it, but there's something in his gaze that hurts my heart. It's at odds with the hardness in his voice. "That happens. All the time. I didn't seek it out, I didn't ask for it. I didn't do anything. For what it's worth, I didn't speak to the first woman. She just gave me the card. And I told you about Leah."

And him saying the name of one of his many lovers slices into me.

"Ryder, maybe I'm not the right person for this job."

"Oh, is that your professional opinion? Because here's my opinion. I'm doing my best, and you're meant to take that and turn it into something that works. It's not about right or wrong in that. You're the best, I want the best and..." He leans back, "we're half way through this. I can't go and find someone else."

He's right. "I'm going to see this through to the end, Ryder. I just get so frustrated. You make the job hard."

"Is this about the job? Or is it about you and me?"

A cold hand squeezes my heart hard. "There's no you and me."

"Bullshit. I can think of a number of things from the other night that says otherwise."

"That was a mistake."

He finishes his martini and another one appears. I don't know if it's the place or the magic pull of Ryder that has the waitress so attentive. "No, it wasn't. And that's what this is about, isn't it? We had sex and you punish me for my past."

I breathe in fast and hard and wrap my fingers around the slender stem of my glass. "It's not your past, Ryder. It's who you are, bone deep, in your DNA."

"I like you, Elliot. Beyond the attraction, the insane chemistry I wasn't expecting; I like you. Do you know how rare that is?"

There's a spark of something bright and light in me, but I squash it down flat because this is Ryder Sinclair and he's not going to change. He might like me and I sure as hell like him, but anything else? No. He's just talking like this because I'm the only access to sex he has for the now.

"I like you, too, Ryder, but that doesn't change anything. And it doesn't change the fact that no matter how well you handled it tonight, you're a magnet to women and you like that role. Now, I need to go."

And without letting him say another word, I get up and leave.

Before my resolve crumbles.

I ran away.

It haunts me because I don't do that. But I don't see how we can get past who and what he is, even if I was stupid enough to believe there was something there.

I do the right thing and throw myself into my work for the next couple of days. Ryder's snowed under, so he says, but there aren't sightings of him in social media and as the minutes tick away and he continues not to bring down any houses, the more my guilt starts to climb.

We're at week three, and it seems the blogs are bored with the fact Ryder has some kind of girlfriend—sorry, fiancée—who is as scandal and newsworthy-free as, well, me. His scandal is milking her relationship, and that's where focus is, the will they won't they no doubt scripted drama being played out with her estranged husband and the Ryder angle has been dropped.

For now.

I'm not foolish enough to buy it's over.

Whether it'll be over for the next two weeks or if the waves will rock back against Ryder and his less than stellar reputation is anyone's guess.

It's one thing I can't control or predict. All I can do is be ready.

Which means I have to put aside the personal crap with us and micro guide.

He has another board meeting coming up. They shifted it around, but he isn't bothered. We talk, but it's mostly via email and text. And...fuck it, I miss him.

I miss him there on my sofa. I miss bickering and talking and laughing and it doesn't matter it's been a thing of my doing along with circumstance, I miss him.

Even when I actually saw him briefly yesterday, it was all business.

I check my watch and start to pack up my desk. Ryder's got a luncheon, one that was thrown at him by the board. The Women's Guild of the Upper West Side.

He's got this, and his mother will be there. Not to mention most of the women will be the matronly sort.

But I don't want to let him go in without my hand guiding him, even if it's just a pep talk and a going over of rules.

Ryder's mother is going to be there and that sends certain warnings going off inside me.

So I close up early and I head to his place.

Ryder throws open the door right as I knock. He's in jeans and a T-shirt, his tattoo on display and his feet are bare. He doesn't smile.

"I'm alone."

"I don't care."

"Yes," he says, "you do."

I narrow my eyes. "Can I come in?"

At that moment, a guy with a fixed gear bike comes up. "Sinclair?"

"Yes." Ryder comes past me and gives the guy some cash and takes the paper bag the man digs out of his insulated messenger bag. Then Ryder just walks past me, wafting the mouth-watering scents of Vietnamese behind him. He pauses at his door. "Come on, Perry. I don't have all morning."

Inside, he heads to the kitchen where I've been once, a masterpiece of charm, industrial and color. "You're eating?"

"I do that," he says. "Along with drinking coffee. You want?"

"It's ten thirty a.m. How the hell did you get Vietnamese at this hour?"

"New York City, baby; that and a lot of money gets results." He sets two cups under his built in espresso machine, inserts some pods and presses a button. Then he moves a pile of papers and his open laptop from the top of the kitchen bench and kicks over a stool to me. "And I'm not going to this thing without eating what I want first. If I'm descending into hell, then I want a stomach full of great food."

Ryder grabs the tiny espresso cups and gives me one, and then he opens the bag and pulls out a banh mi and gives me one half.

"I didn't come here checking up on you," I say, taking a bite and pretty much almost having an orgasm as the flavors hit my tongue. "Oh, my God, this is fantastic."

He smiles low, like he knows what just shot through me. "Best kept secret in Chinatown. Squat, ugly place with zero frills, all thrills in the mouth department, and one of my go-to places."

I take another bite and swallow, the pork melting and spiced just so it melds and builds with the homemade pickles and the herbs. And the hot sauce. The crunch of the bun so light and the inside so soft I'm in heaven. "You're a man of many hidden depths, Ryder. And I mean it. I didn't come to check up."

"Good. Why are you here?"

"Stealing food." Ogling a hot, gorgeous man who has taste... "Doing my job."

"I've been alone. You've been my only downfall."

His words sit in the air, a little too bright and loaded with meaning I don't know how to unpick, or even if I should.

"So, what's your plan for today?"

He shrugs, letting it go. "Get through the whole mind numbing event. I'm going to be scrutinized by my mother, I can tell you that and you've no fucking idea how much that irritates me. Almost as much as..." He trails off then seems to switch tracks. "I'll get through it."

We finish eating, then I say, "I can find the perfect outfit for you."

"Actually, something arrived this morning, which is why I worked from home. I'll be back in fifteen."

He's back in ten minutes and my heart stops beating. The suit is one we decided on for Ryder 2.0. It's dark maroon, so dark it could be black and the perfect level of conservative with a hint of dashing thrown in. The cut's modern, and the tie is rich blues and blacks and he looks good enough to devour slowly.

"You don't need me anymore. It looks better than I imagined."

"I do," he says quietly, gravely. "I need you. I'm glad you're here and we're talking like we used to. So, want to come with me?"

I'm just wearing a pencil skirt with a fitted jacket. I probably look good enough to open a door for him. But he looks at me like I shine.

"I...I have to work. For you."

"This is work," he says with a smile and holds out his arm. "Come on, Perry. Come be bored out of your brain with me. Though, I know with you by my side, that's not going to happen. I like you, Elliot. And, you like me. We work. So...what do you say?"

Chapter Twenty-Three

Ryder

Elliot's face tells me a lot of stories about what I said, and none of them have a happy ending.

Fuck, why the hell did I say we work, and why am I tied up in knots when I'm around her?

She doesn't answer me, simply looks at my arm and starts to tidy the kitchen, putting the papers from the food in the trash and the cups in the dishwasher and through it, the silence grows.

Does she still think I was up to something with those numbers? I should have said something when I saw her, like I'd normally do, make a joke and not get…panicked.

That's not me.

But a lot of this isn't me. Anyone other than Elliot and I'd have just showed them or forgotten them and if found, I'd…yeah, have done things differently. Been me.

Thing is, she thinks I'm some kind of trash. She thinks I'm fickle and shallow and all the things I've never cared about when it comes to someone else. As in my image or what they think. Like me or not, judge me or not, I never cared because I know who I am. I play the field hard when it comes to personal and I work the room harder when it comes to business.

I respect women, I love women. I just never wanted to settle down. Never felt the need to. Never thought about it. And I'm not thinking about it now. No, I'm just thinking about how I look. And it's not good.

Ryder the player. Ryder the man whore. Ryder the fuck boy. In it for nothing more than sensory pleasure and himself. Yeah, I love fucking, I love touching, kissing, I love pleasure. And like most people, of course, I'm into pleasure for myself. But I love giving it, too. Sharing pleasure and a moment with someone. Lots of different someones. Again, it doesn't make me look good.

Yet, I haven't thought about other women in the way Elliot thinks I do, the way I admittedly have before I met her. Sure, I've looked. I'm a guy. It's what we do. But more often than not, I find myself comparing them to her.

Oh, Jesus. I've lost my mind.

It's because I like her and don't simply want to fuck her. I want to talk to her and laugh and spend time with her. No doubt, that's just the spell she weaves, and it'll wear off. Of course it will.

One thing's come from this, and that's I do want to change. Not be a boring bore from boredom world, but someone who garners respect in all aspects of his life. Someone a woman like Elliot would like and respect. Someone a woman like Elliot might want.

I clear my throat. "It's fine, don't worry about it—you don't need to be bored."

"No." She looks at me and smiles. "I want to. Not be bored, go with you. I just need to go home and get changed."

I sweep my gaze over her. "No you don't. You look good, very Elliot."

"Frumpy?"

"You say one thing wrong..." This I can do. And the rest? I'll work on that shit later. And soon she'll be gone and I can see if she wants to be friends, or...yeah. We'll see. But first, I need to be me, the 2.0 version. Fake it until you make it, right? "I don't think you look frumpy at all. I think you look beautiful."

Her smile is hesitant, but it blooms and warmth spreads through me. "It's your lucky day, because today, flattery will get you everywhere. Or a date to this thing."

"Come my lady." I hold my arm out to her once more. "Let's go."

And this time, she takes it.

Thank Christ for the redhead with me. She charms the battleaxes and is a quiet and implacable presence that infuses all around us. And she makes quiet comments that almost make me laugh, which I do back at her until it turns into a game.

But Elliot's on her game, right at the top and she deftly controls anything that might seem like it could go south, like questions. Like the fact my mother brought some kind of beauty queen with her who would have been sitting next to me if it wasn't for Elliot.

And through it all, my fucking mother just smiled her sly little smile.

Over a glass of wine at the fancy bar in pale creams—like the rest of the godforsaken high-end place, I sit with Elliot and rest my elbow on the bar's top.

"To you, Perry." I raise my glass and clink it against hers.

She places her hand against her heart, right between her lovely breasts, hinted at in the lavender button down she's wearing. I remember how they feel and fit my hand, how they taste a little too well.

"Me?"

"You saved me about a billion times."

She takes a sip of her wine and hides a smile behind the rim of the glass. "You did all right, unless you wanted the bait your mom brought in."

"It was a little...on the nose." I slide her a sly look. "But she was hot."

"Your mom?"

"C'mon, Perry, you don't play fair."

How is it that like this we're great?

The word safe wanders through my mind.

This is safe territory.

"Of course I don't. I'm the demon who's going to get you what you want, Sinclair."

"And all I need to do is sell you a part of my soul?"

She wrinkles her nose. "That thing? Nope, I'll stick to the money." Her hand flits across mine and my blood stirs into life at her touch. "You know, Ryder, you did good. You didn't need me today."

"No, but I wanted you." She's staring at me, so I go on. "There. Here. I wanted you here with me."

Her gaze skitters away and I can't shake the feeling I somehow disappointed her, but I'm not sure how. She looked at me like she didn't want me to say what I did.

Women.

I was better off when I didn't care on such a personal level.

Liking someone sucks the big one.

"I'm going to go to the restroom and then I'm getting back to your grindstone." Elliot stands. "I mean, working for you."

And she turns and hurries off.

"I like her."

Mother.

My hand tightens around my glass and I slowly face the diabolical creature. "What's not to like? Elliot's a great person. But I don't think you're lurking—"

"I'm not lurking. I was at the luncheon, dear. I wanted to talk to you, that's all."

"Where's your carrot?"

She takes the seat that Elliot vacated and a gin and elderberry cocktail appears in front of her, courtesy of a suddenly very attentive bartender. My mother loves that drink during day time hours when she has to be at events like this.

"I sent her home."

"At least you didn't pretend not to know what I meant."

"Ryder," she says, "why would I? But you knew I'd bring someone, didn't you? Is that why you enticed Elliot along?"

"Yes." I give her a narrow-eyed glare. "I like to bring a buffer, you know me."

"Sometimes, I don't think I do."

I lean in. "I was being sarcastic, old woman—"

"Ryder."

"—I asked Elliot because she's fun to be around. You remember fun, don't you? Oh, yes, that's right, it's what you do with your sons, have fun at their expense by manipulating Father's letters."

"Watch it, Ryder. I'm your mother, and you're never too old to punish."

I shake my head and laugh, sitting back. "You look spectacular for an old woman."

"You really..." She stops and there's a smile and I know she isn't bothered by my attempt at an insult.

I love her, but she really tests me sometimes, and this whole thing is one big test. "Yeah, I know. Elliot gets pissed off at me, too."

"Does she now? As I said, I like her. A lot. She's smart." She takes a delicate sip of her cocktail. "Don't screw up, Ryder."

"I'm not going to. It's why I have Elliot."

"Oh, darling, you have a lot to learn and so little time." She sighs.

But I'm not going down that path, whatever that is. I have more important fish to go ahead and fry here. Namely, her agenda and how it affects me. "I want to know what's going on."

"I'm your mother. That's what's going on. I'm looking out for you."

"Nope. Not buying it."

She laughs, crossing her legs and toying with her glass. "Hate to break it to you, Ryder, but we share DNA. I'm your mother. I should know, I spent thirty hours in labor. You were not an easy baby to give birth to."

I clench my hand. "You're not funny. And I'm not letting it go. You're up to something. Why the fuck are you taking such an interest in all this, in Father's stipulations?"

"I was named dear, to take part."

"Nope, I mean sure. I get that, but you're taking more of an interest than is needed. Above and beyond, as they say."

"Maybe you need someone to do that. Keep you from screwing up your life. After all, you know you need the help. That's why you hired your pretend girlfriend. No, wait, I think I read fiancée."

I swear, you say something once and it's suddenly etched in stone. "She's not a pretend girlfriend."

"So she's your girlfriend, then? Interesting."

She's goading me. I know she is. And it works. Because I'm pissed off. I hate being manipulated for the pleasures of a dead man and I hate even more my mother seems to be helping that whim for reasons she's not going to tell me. I'd fucking shout where she and the rest of them can stick it—the board, Jenson—if the family company wasn't at stake. And yeah, I want my heirloom, too.

"You know she's not that at all. I don't do girlfriends."

"Pity."

"My life isn't your life, Faye."

She taps her long, tastefully manicured nails against the bar. "I know. But—"

"There are no buts."

"Ryder, I want your life to be fulfilling. And maybe that's why I'm taking an interest. I know you can do your work and live your life the way you want, but one day you might wake up and regret it."

"That's my choice." I also don't think her motives are that altruistic.

She's not out to destroy me or hurt me, I know that. But she likes control. And she's up to something.

"Elliot's very pretty, don't you think?"

"Are you trying to set me up with her? She's not my type. Pretty or plain, it's got nothing to do with me."

I'm lying, but I'm so riled I don't want my mother adding the element of matchmaking to her damn plans. Because no doubt she'll have some dour and boring heiress lined up somewhere for me.

"I'm not about to change. Not for you, and certainly not for some woman I hired."

My mother stares at me, her mouth snapping shut and her gaze shoots just past my shoulder.

My heart sinks like it's suddenly morphed into lead.

I turn.

Elliot's staring at me, too, but it's hurt and vulnerability that flash in her face and it slashes into me.

"I think," she says, "that's my cue to leave."

And she does just that.

Chapter Twenty-Four

ELLIOT

My eyes burn.

"Asshole. Asshat. Bastard."

A litany of insults tumble from me as I stalk out of the restaurant and basically hijack a cab from a rich asshole man who just hailed it.

I don't know if he's an asshole, but he's definitely rich from the cut of his suit, and he's a man, so he's probably an asshole.

When I get back to SoHo, I bypass my office and head straight to my apartment, stripping down and donning pajamas.

As coping mechanisms go, it's that or down a bottle of booze and I don't really think the repercussions of the latter will make me feel good the next day. I try to do some work, but honestly, right now? I can't.

I feel used and that's not fair or right. I'm not being used. That isn't Ryder. And what I overheard wasn't anything I didn't expect, wasn't anything I don't expect.

I'm not his type, I know that. He's not going to change his ways, either, and if he were, not for me. I work for him, just like he said and he's promised me not a damn thing... Yet it all burns. Right down deep where I can't get at it.

"Fuck."

Having sex with him was stupid, I know this. But try as I might, I can't regret it. For a brief, shining moment he wanted me and I want him. I'd have to be an idiot not to want a sample of Ryder Sinclair. After all, everyone else has gotten a piece of him, why not me?

I'm aware how horrible that sounds, what it makes him sound like and that's what I thought he was—a hot piece of man ass to admire and to indulge in if it ever happened. The crush...this is more than a crush, and I don't know what it is except thinking he's a man whore who's good in bed and attached to the prettiest face I've seen on a man is completely wrong and unfair.

Ryder's more than that. Not just in there's a real boy down in the mix. But he's more than what he might seem on the surface, more than the twenty-first century great lover, more than rich and wild and carefree.

He's complex and as much as he frustrates me and gets me riled up at times, I like who he is when he lets himself shine. I like his humor and intelligence and the way he can sound as awkward as a teen. And yeah, I also like that smooth as butter side, too, because it's got substance.

I sigh and flop down on the sofa. Damn him, anyway. "Asshole."

"Elliot?" Ryder. My heart lurches. He's outside my door. I sit completely still. "Perry? I know you're in there."

I don't answer and he starts to knock steadily. It gets louder as he goes. I don't think he's going to go away.

Slowly, I rise from the couch and cross to the door, the floorboards smooth and cool under my bare feet. "In case you didn't notice," I say when I pull the door open by way of greeting, "I left for a reason."

He scowls at me. "It's a little early for a pity pajama party, Perry."

"That's a lot of alliteration."

"Oh you're funny." Beneath the scowl and the anger there's concern and hurt. He pushes past me into my apartment. Then Ryder turns and points. "You ran away."

"You said some shitty things."

He blows out a breath. "To my mother? She's being an interfering busybody. What I do shouldn't be her business. And that goes for who I sleep with, don't sleep with and who I like."

"It's not my business either." I snap the words and go to turn, but he catches my arm. "Let me go."

"So you can run away again? No."

"We're in my apartment. Where am I about to run to, Ryder?" Our gazes clash and the fire in his burns low in my belly.

"Knowing you, you'll think of something."

"I work for you, end of story."

He frowns. "That's not the story, and you know it."

"What is it? Unless you're some kind of out and out liar, what you said comes from truth, just like what I'm saying. I work for you. Nothing more. We had a glitch or whatever you want to call it. So we get through the next two weeks and then off you go, being you."

Ryder doesn't speak. He lets me go and rubs a hand over his face. "That's what it is, huh?"

"Yes."

"I call bullshit."

I raise my hands. "You don't get to call bullshit on unfettered truth."

"Well, apart from the glitch as you call it, that isn't the truth. We don't have a working relationship. At least, not for me. It's something else. And because it's something else, it's personal."

I don't want to do this. I take a step back and he follows. "Client and make over queen, right here."

"No, Elliot. This is you and me. We're more than client and make over magic queen. Apart from anything else, I thought we were friends."

"You don't do friendship with women."

"Not fair, Perry. I've told you I see you as a friend. You might be my only female friend—I don't count my brothers' significant others because that's a different beast—but I know a friend. And if our friendship is way more complicated than others, so be it. But I see you as a friend."

It's the fucking story of my life. Friend zone. And I know that's not exactly what he's saying to me. But what am I meant to think? That he's gone and lost his mind and fallen in love with me? Because that's a dangerous and fantasy-riddled path that has nothing to do with reality.

"But we're not friends. You slept with me, that's all."

"I think there were two people involved, Elliot," he says, tapping his foot on the floor. "And I'm not talking friends with benefits or fuck buddy bullshit. I'm talking you and me and how I feel and what it is I want."

"Yeah?" I ask. "And what's that?"

"You."

His quiet word knifes through me.

"Only because there's no one else." I glare at him.

Ryder glares back. "You don't think I know my own mind, Elliot?"

"I'm here. There's no one else accessible."

"Bullshit. If I wanted, I'd find a way. I'm trying to clean up my act to the world but you don't think, if I wanted to get down and dirty and didn't want you, that I'd find a way with some other babe?" He stalks up, closing the gap I made and this time I stand my ground.

"Do you hear yourself?"

"I do, actually. I don't get you. You're this powerhouse. You're beyond intelligent and competent and you have class that can't be bought." He pokes me with a finger. "You're confident, and then when it comes to me you think I just want you for no other reason than there's a fucking vulva available?"

"I didn't say that!" I poke him right back.

He's even closer now and I shiver from the heat of him. "You didn't have to. It's in your actions and words."

"What do you expect from me, Ryder? Look at you and look at me."

"I'm looking," he says, sliding his hands down my arms. "And usually I like what I see. What's so hard to believe about that?"

Everything. Nothing. A bolt of fury, of fear, shoots through me. "You want me because you've been without, that's what the you and me thing is."

"You know fuck all. I want you for you. I'll show you."

And he kisses me. Hard. Carnal. It's an angry kiss and I want that. Because I'm angry, too. At myself for being everything he said. At him for being Ryder. And I need him right now.

I go to break the kiss, and I push him, but somehow my hands slide up his chest and neck, and I grab his hair, tangling my fingers in the thick, soft locks and pull him harder into me.

"I should wring your neck," he mutters, kissing and sucking a path down my throat as one of his hands delve down into my pajama bottoms. He grabs my ass and hauls me against his hard on.

I grind against him. My hand is still in his, and I rake the nails of my other over his shirt, under his overcoat and suit jacket. "I should punch you."

"Fuck, you're violent, Perry. I like it."

"You're an asshole." And he slips a finger down between the cheeks of my ass and up along my slit from behind, and my body explodes into a cascade of pleasure and need.

He claims my mouth again. The kiss is hard. Tongue, teeth, lips. It's sex.

And he takes me, turns me so I'm against him, my back pressed into him, and now his fingers play my pussy from the front, teasing, down over the outer lips, each side, and this man knows his female anatomy. He knows where the clitoris reaches beneath the skin and even as he plays the nub, he works those sensitive lips, the indent each side that's full so many pleasure receptors I'd be boneless and on the ground if he wasn't holding me up.

"You're so fucking stubborn, Perry," Ryder says against my ear, over the pants and gasps and moans coming from me as my heart jack rabbits and I'm completely burning for more of him. He bites and licks my earlobe. "You shine, and I want you. Do you want me?"

"Yes."

He kisses lower, over my nape, and bites me there, making me squeal as he pushes a finger in me. "You want me to push you on the sofa and fuck your brains out?"

"Yes, damn you, yes."

I want anything he'll do to me.

He lets me go and gives me a shove and I land on the sofa, grabbing the back with my hands as I try to get my balance.

But Ryder isn't going to let me. He's there. Hands on me, over me. And as he kisses my neck, there's a soft shift of material, the hiss of a zipper and I try to turn, but he stops me with his mouth against my cheek. "No."

Ryder moves back a little and then pulls my bottoms down, and the cool air touches and teases my wetness. He's left my underwear on. He hooks a finger against the gusset and pulls it to one side.

"Ryder?"

"I'm admiring the work of art you are, Elliot. Gorgeous. Pink and beckoning. Made for me, I think."

And the head of his cock is there, pressing at me. It isn't a pretty lovemaking, or seduction. It's raw and angry and full of jagged erotic pleasure. And I want it all. I beg for it. I meet him thrust for thrust and it's wild.

The deep singing pressure inside builds and I come and then he starts to hammer into me, hard, deep, relentless and then finally he sets me off once more, right as he comes and we tumble down into dark ecstasy together.

Chapter Twenty-Five

RYDER

The silence afterwards is broken only by the whispery sounds of us putting clothes back to right and I want to kick myself. Hard.

"Elliot," I say.

She won't look at me, and her cheeks are flushed and her hands shake as she smooths them over her hair, pulling it back like she wants to tie that red bountiful beauty up. Hide it away.

"If you apologize, I'll kill you."

I half smile. "I didn't mean for that to happen."

Her gaze shoots to me. "That's dangerously close to an apology."

"I'm not apologizing for great sex." I'm still dressed and after a moment's hesitation I strip out of my overcoat. My head's still slightly dazed and the thrum of the orgasm and its pleasure still ricochets through me. But I lay the coat down on the armchair and sit because I'm a little unsteady, and I'm in half a mind to reach for her again.

Or walk out the fucking door and into the nearest bar.

"Then, it's me?"

"You think I'm saying I didn't mean that to happen because of you?"

"I'm better than just being something to warm your dick."

I laugh. It's not a pretty sound and I don't feel warm and fuzzy inside. This thing with us gets real complicated, real fast, and I can't for the life of me work out why. It's like we both want something, or don't want something, that's slightly out of reach.

And the more I think about it, try to find an answer, the more slippery it becomes.

I wait until she glares at me, but the vulnerable light, the hopeful light, along with the shadows of no that are there are the things that sink in deep. The anger is nothing more than a byproduct of the mess of emotion she feels. I know, because I feel that mess, too.

"There are plenty of places to warm my dick, as you so charmingly put it. And one of them doesn't even require another person. Actually, if I got all creative, there are a few that don't require anyone else, although I haven't tried those."

I'm getting off track.

"So you didn't mean for that to happen and it happened?"

"Contrary to what's in your head, I find you hard to resist."

She sinks down on the couch, at the other end. The whole piece of furniture is askew, a taunt of what happened. "What are we doing?"

"I don't know."

And I don't.

I'm fucking pissed off at myself for fucking her because I like her. She's my friend and maybe she's more than that, too. A friend and not a friend. Beyond just friends. It's confusing. Like everything else to do with her.

"You wouldn't ever be satisfied with one woman, Ryder."

"I've never tried. Is that where we are?"

"No. I'm nipping this now because you won't go there, and I don't want to."

"Because you think I can't do just one woman?"

"Not think," she says softly. "Know."

Maybe she's got a point. Women want me, always have, and I don't see it changing. And I want them. I like the variety, I like having sex and all the sex I've had before—including the sex that led to me being here, the scandal—has been uncomplicated. Simple, unfettered, sex.

This?

This is complicated.

Complex and intricate and full of minefields I don't expect.

And the sex is out of this world. I want to spend time exploring her. I want to worship. I want to fight and laugh and fuck her just as hard as I did then. And I want all the stuff outside the sex, too.

But what that entails is anyone's guess. Or, I should say, mine. Because this is so uncharted it's something I didn't know even existed.

Elliot's phone pings and she grabs it from the coffee table, opens it and reads the message. She stands suddenly and smooths her hands through her hair again. "Since you're here, we need to get you prepped."

"Prepped?"

"Your last week is going to be as CEO with—"

"I'm doing what now?" I pull out my phone and the only messages are from my brothers all angling to know if I've slept with Elliot, slept with anyone else, and advice on how to stay on the straight and narrow.

Really what I need.

I ignore them and go to my emails, but there's nothing there either. And my diabolical parent didn't seem fit to tell me this today. She'd have known.

Elliot frowns but there's relief there, because she's got something else to focus on other than the hot sex that just happened. I feel like the male version of fucking Alice right about now.

"No one told you?"

"Not even you."

"I thought you knew. I just got the message as a reminder for you from your mom."

Fuck me, I want to break something. "My mother has your number now?" I hold up a hand before she can answer me. "Where there's a way there's my mother. Of course she does. And no, that reminder is the only message. Trust me, at least on this."

"I trust you," she says quietly.

"Just not with sex and relationship things."

She shoots me a long, cool look. "Let's concentrate on what we need to do for you to be there tomorrow morning." Elliot hurries over to the beautiful small art deco desk in one corner that looks more for display than use, but of course, she uses it. She picks up her laptop and comes back over, sitting and opening it. "You might as well sit down. Let's get started."

So I sit.

No one can tell me I'm not getting my money's worth with Elliot. Three nights ago, when I finally left her place at some ungodly hour of the morning, I felt like I'd been deprogrammed. No stone was left unturned within me.

She told me what to wear, how to act, and then made me go through that. She threw out scenarios, riled me, pissed me off; and each time I started to run my mouth, she stopped me.

And...she did an amazing job. Every time I've been thrown some curve ball, I handle it like the kind of responsible, boring adult they want. I'm doing shit I have people for in my own work because this stuff isn't for me, and it isn't for the CEO. I'm being tested.

There's still one more meeting coming up, and I know when I'm given a hot sex pot as a receptionist who's, ah, very open to other things, it isn't the test. It's other women when I'm invited out at night and I go, but always bow out early. I report in to Elliot and...

I want to see her.

I can't deny that.

She calls to me and it's not just sex. This is different, but fuck me if I can work out why.

Objectively, I know hotter women exist. But she does something to me. And this woman I once thought plain with an intriguing mouth sets me alight just thinking about her.

I'm meant to be out tonight, but instead, I'm haunting my loft like a horny, frustrated ghost.

Running my hand over one of my guitars, an old battered thing that is beautiful because it was something I bought years ago. It belonged to Long Johnny Slim, one of the best old school Chicago blues men no one outside that scene has heard of. I rarely play it because I don't have his talent, but the cheap guitar was gold in his hands.

I think about playing something, but I'm not in the mood.

One weird thing has been happening.

Lacey Fox. She of the scandal that landed me here has been texting. I put it down to dear old mother testing me. I just delete the messages without reading. I'm not falling for anything that obvious.

My phone rings and it's my mother, so I ignore her.

Thing is, I decide as I flop down on the couch, I don't want to lose Elliot. I don't want to lose her from my life and right now, I'm thinking I'll take her anyway I can get her. But what if sex—more sex—with her means I lose her in the end?

I don't want to lose that friendship. I don't want to lose the closeness I have with her, the way I can be open with her. That openness that comes from her, too, in those brilliant flashing moments we have.

In a perfect world, I'd throw in, I'd ask for it all, and give her everything she could ever want, including me, because it comes to me that she might feel very much the same about me as I do about her.

Whatever that is, screams, sings, coos, whispers 'more'.

But I also know myself.

I'm not a good man in that respect.

In bed? I'm great.

Flirting? I'm winning gold stars.

I've got seduction and making a woman feel like the only woman worth anything and leaving her still feeling good about herself down pat.

The long haul I have doubts. Huge ones. I've never done that.

And what if I get her? What if I get her and we go deep into whatever this thing is and I'm me? Being me, I'd fuck it up by fucking someone else because they catch my eye. It doesn't matter I haven't seen anyone since I met Elliot I want to fuck. I might just be the screw up dear old dead Dad and the rest think I am.

If I'm that, then Elliot's better off without me.

There are a few days left. Lacey still contacts me and I ignore her. And the more I do, I know these last days are critical.

What if she goes to the press?

I find myself online, reading about me, something I never do and I'm gobsmacked.

Elliot might be a goddess. A magical one.

Because the man I'm reading about looks like me, sounds like me if I was reformed, upstanding, responsible. I take things seriously. I've gone from a bad boy to a man women swoon over because he's in love.

I don't think the in love part is from her, that's the interpretation from the photos of me and Elliot. Of how I look at her. Of what can only be the carefully orchestrated exchanges overheard, even when we argued. We look like a real couple.

And of course Elliot is everything they say she is. Smart, together, career woman, steady, scandal free.

Oh, they miss the nuances that really make Elliot special. Her wicked streak, her humor, her sharp tongue. And they don't know how she kisses, either. Obviously.

I drag in a breath.

There's one more event that's super important to go to tomorrow night, but that's not why I leave work at the company early. That's not why I hightail it across town to SoHo and breeze past Lena and into Elliot's gorgeous office.

God, she looks good.

It's a different kind of suit she has on, and her hair is still pinned back, but there's something so understated and hot about it all I'm weak at the knees, and my cock stirs.

She looks up. "Can I call you back?" she asks whoever's on her phone over her Bluetooth. Then she hits end on her phone, pulls the earpiece out, and says, "is something wrong? Shouldn't you be at Sinclair's, dazzling them?"

"I have." I wave a hand in the air like it isn't important I reach my goals, and for a moment that's true. "You are a master at what you do."

"Excuse me?"

"I just read everything about me online and I'm impressed."

She frowns, even though her mouth quirks. "You just did a very Ryder thing by leaving work to come here to tell me the job I've been doing to make you not look like the Ryder who walked out of the important CEO job is brilliant?"

"Yes."

Elliot laughs. "Ryder. You're hopeless."

I don't laugh. I don't laugh at all. "Elliot."

The laughter dies. "What is it?"

"I've been thinking." I rub a hand over the back of my neck; a pimpled teen gathering the strength to ask the school beauty queen out. "I...there's only a few days left."

"I know that."

"And I just, well, you and me. I think there's more to it than a passing attraction. More than just being friends. And maybe we should, you know..."

Elliot Perry looks at me and crosses her arms.

"No."

Chapter Twenty-Six

ELLIOT

I don't know who's more flabbergasted at that. Me or him.

His nervous demeanor almost got me, it did, and I want the offer than he almost put into words.

But if he can't say it...

I'm worth more than that half-assed offer of a maybe something more. Whatever that means.

I might not be the prettiest, and he might be the hottest man ever, but if he can't, then I won't.

It's that devastating. That simple. That complicated.

"What do you mean no?"

I'm so glad the desk lies between us. It's a cool afternoon, but cloudless and the light coming in through my window in my office lights his face and he's perfection itself. And I know I had to say no.

This is going to hurt, but it's for him as much as it is for me. "Ryder, you've worked so damn hard, and you have become different in a way, but that big a change for real isn't happening overnight or in four weeks, not really. And you...you don't really want me."

"You don't know that."

"Ryder, you've bonded with me. It happens."

His eyes narrow and he slides his hands into the pockets of his trousers. "So you fuck all your clients?"

"It's a special service," I snap. "No, only you, and I shouldn't have done that, but you're a very hot man and I was stupid."

"Stupid is one way to put it."

Shit, I'm mangling this. "What I'm trying to say is what I've been saying all along. You bonded, and you only want me because there are no other women."

"Okay. I'm sure you're right," he says suddenly, like it doesn't matter, like he wasn't wanting more. And maybe he's just relieved I stopped the nonsense. "Friends, right?"

I don't want to say no way in hell can I be friends with him, but I smile. "Friends."

"I better get back to work." He turns and heads to the door. But Ryder stops and spins to face me. "Oh, yeah, one thing, tomorrow night's that big event. It's a Sinclair fucking fundraiser. I don't even know what for. Probably a host of good causes. All in my father's honor. One last outing for us. You're coming, right?"

"Sure." This thing's in my calendar. No way am I letting Ryder go by himself. Not that I think he can't handle it, because actually, I do. But because I'm selfish and weak and want that last big night with him where a small part of me can pretend we're together.

"Thank God. I hate those things. High end, conservative, rich—wall to wall—the kind you haven't yet seen. Well, maybe you have, but not on this scale. There's no art or weird old rich people in amazing outfits with fuzzy pink dogs on their heads."

Suddenly I laugh, that old lady at the art show coming into my head. I liked her. She didn't give a fuck about anyone or anything. "I can bring the dog hats."

"I don't think they'll approve at this kind of event. Boring music, boring food, boring drinks, boring people, boring speeches, and boring back patting at doing something for the world. Usually, I avoid these like the plague."

We're playing a game, I realize. Pretending things are all fine and dandy with us both.

"I can't wait," I say. "You sell it."

"See you tomorrow."

And then he's gone.

I don't know why, but I want to cry.

I'm such an idiot.

We're halfway through the evening at the fundraiser and I'm beginning to think Ryder oversold it.

I manage to get him away from some old man who's droning on. Ryder runs the backs of his fingers down along my exposed spine on the long evening dress I wear and I shiver, my blood sparking. "Thank you for saving me," he murmurs, his lips not quite brushing my ear. "I thought I'd have to poke an eye out with a fork. Not one of his, unfortunately, one of mine, just to get out of here."

"Think of what's almost in your grasp."

"I am."

And I shiver again, because there's a hidden depth of meaning in his words that I want to hold to me more than anything.

"Ryder..." I breathe out his name as a warning, but it comes out more like a litany.

"What do you say we get out of here before the demon of boredom eats our souls?"

I laugh. "You're not thinking straight."

"I am. And no one's going to penalize me for going early with you. After all, you're my fake fiancée."

"Don't say that again, and I'm out the door with you."

"Consider the fake engagement done."

"Where are we going?" I ask.

"It's a surprise."

And Ryder leads me out the door and into the night.

Brooklyn. Smith Street. We're completely overdressed, but somehow, it's okay. Ryder takes my hand as we step from the car and he leads me to a building.

He knocks and a little slot opens. Then he hands over what looks like two coins. And he says the words, "Honey and the Bee."

The slot snaps shut and the door opens and we enter a long, dark corridor that leads to a set of steps that wind down. Music and laughter wafts up, growing louder as we go.

"Ryder, where have you taken me?"

But I think I know.

When the man opens the door down at the bottom of the stairs, we step into the luxuriously darkly red wallpapered and velvet seated bar, complete with a stage and a band. Nothing like the one I took him to. This is barebones, and it's all wonderful.

"It's a speakeasy. How…?"

He grins. "I looked into it. And I liked where you took me so much I wanted to find somewhere to share with you."

"You did?" I grin back, I can't help it. The place is something I never knew existed and I'm in love.

With the place.

Not with Ryder.

Oh, God, definitely not that.

It would be a disaster.

But he doesn't let me sit with those thoughts, instead he makes me dance, holding me close, just there in front of a table. No one else is dancing but with the music and Ryder looking at me like I'm all that exists, I don't care.

I'll take the moment and run.

He spins me out and then back in again, right up against his hard, warm body and my heart's beating wild and fast and erratic and everything is humming inside with the sweetest kind of electricity.

I can barely breathe because everything is taken up by him.

We finally stop dancing—we're swaying now, his hands low on my back, mine flat on his chest—as the music ends, but he doesn't release me.

"I do like you, Elliot. A whole fucking lot."

I'm a coward and everything inside lurches like he sees into me, down past everything to my soul, and I can't speak. The world shifts and tilts and my stomach is a wild sea. I drop my head against his chest and breathe in his intoxicating scent as he whispers fingers against my nape, beneath my hair.

I like him, too. More than like him. The other L word comes into my head, but I don't give it purchase.

"Sit?"

"Sounds like a plan." I raise my head and find my smile again.

He releases me and we find a table. The light is low in here, like shining bronze and the shadows deep and inviting. I sit, grateful not to be on my unsteady legs and I can't help but think maybe there's a chance for us, but I push it away as he goes to get drinks from the bar.

As he crosses the room, eyes follow him. A woman peels away from her friends and into his path and he bends his head, his hand on her arm. He smiles but shakes his head.

The reason why it wouldn't work. So much temptation for a man like him. The pick of everything.

On his way back, a hot young guy comes up to him and he does the same thing. The hand on the arm, the smile, the shake of his head.

"It's a wild honey and blood orange mescal cocktail. The bartender swears it's good."

I take a sip and it is, but, as we drink and chat, I suddenly blurt out, "Is that what it's always like for you?"

"What?"

"People thinking they can proposition?"

"I turned her down." His gaze holds mine, the dark melting chocolate inviting. "Him, too."

"I saw that. I wasn't...wasn't accusing, just curious, I guess."

Ryder shrugs. "It happens. It's fine."

I just nod.

"Listen, Elliot, it's part of life. It happens to you, it happens to everyone. Half the people that hit on me wouldn't if they weren't cruising, weren't out drinking. If I'm in a store, I mostly don't get hit on."

Suddenly I start laughing. "Mostly."

"What?" He frowns.

"Only you could make it seem like it's not a thing."

"It isn't." He leans forward. "I like you, I told you that. You don't really believe me, so I can't do a thing other than offer my friendship and an open door. I don't want these people."

Ryder stands, taking the last swallow of his drink and I think he's off to the bar, but instead, he goes to the stage area where the small band is. They're getting ready to perform and no doubt Ryder's just requesting a song.

A guy comes up and gestures to the seat, pulling it out and putting his glass on the lacquered surface.

"It's taken," I say.

He shrugs and moves on as someone strums the guitar.

I don't know what makes me look over. But I do and there, head bent over the guitar, is Ryder. I'm on my feet before I know what I'm doing as he plays some rusty notes.

He starts to sing. The song is pretty, folksy and full of heart. His voice is low with a hint of gravel. It's nothing to write home about but the tune and the words and the way he looks at me as he sings about unrequited love, about offering that love open handed, open-hearted is.

It's the most beautiful thing I've heard and seen.

And I can't move.

When the band starts up and the singer joins in, Ryder hands the guitar to the owner and comes over to me. He looks down into my eyes and he's not smiling.

Intensity thickens the air.

"That's how I feel, Elliot. About you."

If there's a glimmer of a chance, I want it. I want him.

I go up on my toes and kiss him.

Ryder's arms come about me. His lips part, and the kiss is like the song.

Then he lifts his head.

"Let's get out of here," he says.

Chapter Twenty-Seven

RYDER

I undress Elliot slowly in my bedroom, under the low, liquid gold light from the lamps and she's so beautiful.

Taking my time, kissing her as I go, I worship every piece of flesh I expose. We don't speak, not since she said yes to me in the car here, and the ride is a blur of heat and kisses and anticipation and need that still rocks me to my core.

But we don't need words right now.

Her breasts react under my touch, the nipples beading and tiny goosebumps appear as I trace a path over her ribcage. Elliot makes a tiny sound that, in turn, gets me even harder than I am, but I ignore my physical reaction. I want to immerse myself in her, slowly, completely.

I kiss a path down her body, laving each nipple with my tongue. Her hands come out and grasp me and I keep moving down.

The dress is unzipped, at her hips, and I trail my fingers over the soft swell of her stomach, then I kiss and lick the skin, grazing with my teeth.

Her gardenia scent is twined with arousal and it's the hottest thing I've ever had the privilege of inhaling.

I lift my head, looking up and her lip is half caught between her teeth, a blush spreading like blooming flowers over her flesh and her eyes are half shut. She's an erotic painting, living art, and I drink it in, that image. I horde it deep for safekeeping. And then I rest back on my heels as I pull the dress over her hips.

That juncture, where her pussy lies beneath the scrap of lace and cotton, is damp, and I want it. But more, I want her to be so aroused she's lost in the moment. I want to see the pleasure rise and I want to explore her taste and heat and wetness. Learn all there is to know about her.

I suspect that will take a lifetime, and right now, that lifetime is worth taking, worth giving, sharing.

Sliding my palm over her pubis, I move down and her thighs part. I push my fingers along each side of the edge of her panties there and oh, yeah, she's wet. I feel that on my flesh and it makes my hard on almost painful.

But it's a knife edge of pleasure and pain and anticipation and I remove my hand, pulling her panties down so I can see her. She's so fucking gorgeous. Those private lips invite and taunt with their dusky color. The line of red downy hair that leads up from where the hood of her clitoris pokes out is sweet. I run my tongue over her there and she cries out, a wavery sound that heads straight south. I lick and kiss and taste, I push my tongue into her, and then I part those lips and slide my finger in, exploring slowly that tight, hot hole.

Her fingers bite hard into my shoulder and she starts to shake, her orgasm coming in, a roll of contractions and she's gasping, saying my name and then I rise up and she wraps about me, her eyes unfocused, and we kiss, sharing her taste.

I let her strip me, her fingers shaking as she touches and explores. And she sinks down, fingertips dancing along my cock.

"Oh, fuck me."

My entire body jerks with electric pleasure as her mouth closes over the head of my cock and she sucks me in, down deep to the back of her throat. I want to tell her to stop, I want to fuck her mouth hard. It takes every single drop of willpower I have not to do a damn thing and let her explore me.

She sucks and uses her hand, wrapping it at the base and pulling me back and forth, going so deep with her mouth she's at her hand, and the base of my cock, and then she's back, teasing the head, her hand working me and—

"I'm gonna come, you need to stop."

She doesn't. Elliot, that evil, wonderful woman that she is, keeps going and as the need pushes me, I come as she takes me all the way in and I almost black out from the hard waves of pleasure that hit me.

Then I have her, pulling her into my arms and I'm kissing her so hard, mouths open, tongues mating in a wild dance.

The kiss slows, morphing back down into slow seduction then back up into urgent need, and I take her to the bed.

I cover her body with mine, her thighs wide, her hips rising up, her sex on offer, and I can't believe I'm hard already. All over again.

I slowly enter her and we make love. It's the only way to describe that coming together. It's not sex. It's something more. Soft gasps and low moans. A merging of flesh and emotion and I could do this forever, too.

It's just pure pleasure, building and rebuilding of the urgency, almost reaching the peak until one of us backs down. A tease, a not wanting this to stop.

I don't know how long we do this, but sometimes she's riding me, sometimes I'm rocking into her, and finally, finally there's no way back down, only up and over that edge into pure, intense orgasmic bliss that seems to never end.

After we lay there, just breathing, sprawled and tangled together.

"That was," she says, "wow."

"I think it might have been all capital letters kind of wow." I kiss her nose, then her lips. "And I don't want to stop. I just need a few."

She laughs and draws patterns on my chest. "It's one for the books."

"It's a three-volume novel."

Later, we have sex again and finally fall asleep. I'm too exhausted to go again.

I wake to soft fingers tracing the tattoo on my back.

"I've created a monster," I mutter.

"I'm touching, that's all." But she sounds satisfied. "This whole tattoo, it's to do with your arm, isn't it? Definitely The Divine Comedy."

"It's life. That man in Dante's epic visits hell, purgatory, and paradise. One without the rest isn't living. To appreciate things, you need to know the others."

"All this and you really do play guitar."

"Boarding school. I think I took up guitar as a fuck you to the old man. I'd tell him I was going to join a band, not go into business."

She laughs. "Did he like that?"

"Not really, but he knew I wouldn't. Piano was one thing, but the guitar he saw as a waste of time."

"And your mom?"

"Whatever made us happy, really. But they were empty words on my part. I'm definitely not good enough. It's the hell of the pleasure, knowing you'll never be as good as you want to be."

"And here I thought it was all a way to impress girls."

I pull her over me and roll us so I'm on my back and she's on me. It's a position I'm fast loving with her. Any position is one I'm fast loving with her. Any at all. "There was that." I give her a long look. "Did I impress you, Perry?"

"You got me here, so yeah."

She leans down and kisses me and I'm hard all over again. I take her hips, moving her so her pussy slides against me. And she shivers and moans. "More?"

"Yes, Ryder, I want more."

And I push up into her and we start all over again.

It's gray in the morning when I get up.

Elliot's still asleep and I watch her for a long time, just standing there. Her red hair is tangled out over the pillows on my charcoal-colored bedding and her pale skin and one rosy nipple peek out and it's all I can do not to get back in that bed.

Instead, I go down and make coffee.

I don't know what happened. I really don't. But even now I can't shake the fact it wasn't just sex.

Sipping my espresso, I check my phone. A message from my mother stating privately everyone's impressed. And I know I'll probably get everything I thought I wanted because of Elliot.

Except maybe Elliot.

The best sex of my life that keeps getting better, that's what it is. And she's the kind of woman on the surface who is perfection for the image she created for me. The Elliot below? Actually perfect for me how I am.

Perfect, that is, if I wasn't a fuck up in the way she's accused me of being. I've never had a girlfriend. A relationship that lasted beyond the bedroom and some good times out of it. And here I am, looking at a woman built for relationships, built for the forever thing.

This sex that's more than sex, this sex that reaches down to the marrow, to cellular level, it changes everything and nothing.

If I go forward with this, if I pursue her the way I have been, after last night...I'm not going to just hurt me, I'll hurt her. If we go further, it will be the kind of hurt that leaves deep scars.

I'll fuck up, I know I will. Somehow, someway, I'll stumble, sleep with someone else because, realistically, how long can this thing with me only wanting her last?

I'll do something and I'll lose her.

Better to lose her now.

Elliot chooses that moment to appear and she's so soft and sleep fuzzed and wearing not much at all except a T-shirt she found in my room that leaves all kinds of interesting things hinted at, right there at the top of her thighs. I don't think. I just take.

I fuck her on the bench and it's hot. And after, we spend the morning laughing and talking and touching until finally she moves away when I reach for her.

"You have to go to work, Sinclair."

We're not talking about it, which is good. But we're going to have to, and...shit.

"I don't mind taking the day off."

"After all the work I put in? You're going. Do—do you want to hang out tonight?"

"Sure."

And we make arrangements for a nice little upscale bar that's nearby.

Maybe the talk can wait, maybe I can get another few days of Elliot to cram into my memories.

Elliot isn't there when I arrive at the bar, and the doubts creep in as a beautiful woman comes up and flirts with me and it's easy to flirt back because it doesn't mean anything.

I could have her.

I know that.

But I don't want her.

I want Elliot.

Yet…yet…everything from that morning is there in my head and Elliot deserves better than me.

Elliot enters the bar and I decide to just do it. Rip the band aid off. This isn't love, right? It's just lust getting all confused in the intimacy of friendship, of the sweetness and pull of Elliot herself.

One day, I'll slip up. So I might as well pretend it's today.

I'm such a fucking bastard, and I feel dirty and low and I turn up the flirt, all while Elliot approaches.

"Ryder."

I turn to her. "You're right. About me. I can't change, so it's best we forget last night."

Elliot just stares at me. No shock. No nothing except contempt and dignity and something inside me breaks.

"You're a fucking coward."

She turns and walks out.

The woman next to me is, I think, talking, but she's nothing more than a buzzing fly.

Everything hurts.

I've just made the biggest mistake in my life.

Chapter Twenty-Eight

ELLIOT

Fury, hot and wild, storms through me as I stalk out of the damn bar and toward Prince Street.

I shove past people, vision blurred as something bitter rises in my throat, threatening to choke me.

He's a coward, pure and simple. I don't know what game the man's playing, but I don't deserve it. I don't deserve him. I deserve better than a man who sees me and then deliberately flirts with someone else.

"Elliot."

His voice wraps around me, the urgent note going for my heart, but I harden that stupid, stupid part and keep going.

"Elliot. Wait, damn it."

I don't stop. I'm at my building, and inside so fast I almost sob with relief.

But I don't because my skin starts to prickle as the door slams shut a moment or two too late.

"I said wait."

I whirl around, hating his beautiful face in that moment. Hating all the things he made me feel, all the things he enticed me to believe, all the hope he stirred, only to smash it all to pieces with one cowardly act with a side serve of careless words.

A few people are still in the building and I turn away from him and head to the stairs, Ryder hot on my heels.

If I can't shake him, I still have a job to do, so I'd rather we fight away from everyone else.

I'd rather not see the bastard at all.

He's there, behind me, swearing, and I just race up the steps. It's not until I'm on the second floor landing in the stairwell he grabs me. I snatch my arm back. "Go away, Ryder. I'm sure there are some women in the world left for you to fuck."

"I deserved that."

The bitterness bubbles over like acid. "Oh, you do, do you? Would you like a medal?"

"No. Damn it, please, I'm sorry."

But I back away from him as he reaches for me again and I shake my head. "All these women? All these beautiful, gorgeous women who keep throwing themselves at you, and you sleep with me."

"I didn't want her, Elliot. I was..." He doesn't finish it, but heat flares high in his lean cheeks. On his throat is a mark from my mouth last night.

It punches me hard in the stomach. And the memories roll through me, hard and fast and unwanted.

I'll never be able to get rid of them, I realize. No matter how much I want to. They're all lasered deep in my brain. In my heart. And I...

I don't just have a crush on him.

This involves my blood, my bones, my heart.

I hate him.

I want to cry.

Instead, I nod. "Was what? You can't finish that, can you? Because it dawned on you, all these women and you've been sleeping with me. And it hit you, didn't it? What it would mean if we kept doing that."

He closes his eyes and my heart somehow hurts even more. "Because you're the only one."

Ryder doesn't explain what that means. And all kinds of thoughts jumble through my head. From hopeful to desperate to full of despair.

"Yeah, and it hit you."

"Yep." He takes a breath and pushes his hair from his face, looking all levels of disgusted. "It did."

Like that, I know it's over. Just like that.

"You got all caught up in it all, Ryder," I say, a terrible weariness weighing down my words as I grip the painted iron handrail because if I don't my knees might buckle. "You slept with me because I was the only one you could access during this. Just like I said before."

I turn and push open the exit door to the floor and go to my office, unlocking the door.

"That's not true."

Of course he's still there. Ryder's tenacious and stubborn and even if I hate him, he's still the most beautiful man I've ever seen. Funny, I thought once the gloss of him came off I'd see him differently. But he's still him.

He just doesn't really want me and he went all ham fisted about ending it.

At least we'll have Paris. I almost laugh at the clichéd line. But I can't because this isn't funny at all.

"It is and we both know it."

"I don't know why I flirted with her, I wasn't into her at all, Elliot."

I suck in a breath. "You said. And yet, you did. And I got the message, loud and clear."

He closes the door to the office and in the semidarkness of my closed offices, he leans back against the wall, hands behind his back, eyes shut.

Tired.

Tired and beautiful, a fallen angel, like something from his tattoos on his back. Except that's me putting it on him. Because this isn't real conflict. It's him being his version of decent. He thinks he's conflicted because he isn't someone who doesn't care. He isn't someone who's indifferent or worse, likes to cause pain.

Ryder doesn't want me, but he wants me to feel better. And that, I think might make it all worse.

"I get it," I say. "Like I've said, I get it."

His eyes snap open and he looks at me steadily, but doesn't say a word. There's something there in his eyes I don't quite get, but if it was a thing for me to hold on to, a thing to give me hope, he'd tell me. He'd fight.

And in that tiny moment I want that. I want a man to fight for me. To prove he wants me.

"You don't."

"Ryder..." I go to the desk where Lena sits and open a drawer. "I was easy access for a man like you."

"No, you were difficult, are difficult. I fucked up. I know that. I thought—it doesn't matter what I thought. I just figured you should have better."

I nod. "Because you'll fuck up? You won't change?"

"And if I don't?"

"Ryder, what is that meant to mean? Are you offering yourself to me as some kind of experiment? To see if you can keep sleeping with one woman, maybe see if you can form a relationship?"

"I think I might be. Elliot—"

"Because that's a really half-assed, one foot out the door, selfish jerk move. I deserve better than that. I was easy access, but that access is gone. You go do you, Ryder. Really. I'm sure there are other women out there you can run your little experiment or trial on."

"So you're done? That it?" He straightens, frowning.

And I dig in the drawer for the keys I keep in a small box in there. I wrap my fingers around it and look down. "I think so. With you and me."

There's a silence but then he moves. I feel more than hear him approach. "No one else...no one out there is you, Elliot. I might want to fuck someone else, but I don't want to hang out with them like I do you."

Fucking asshole. My fingers tighten on the box and I look furiously up at him.

He meets my gaze. "That may have come out wrong."

"Or right. Here. You go do you." I hand him the keys.

"I didn't mean that. I didn't mean I want to fuck other people. I meant if I did, I—"

"Ryder, stop. You're making things worse."

He looks down at the keys I pulled from the box. "I don't understand."

"The board's decision is going to be made soon, but you can't just snap back to the old Ryder. Not right away. That's just begging for you to lose it all. I think they call it snatching defeat from the jaws of victory."

I'm running on professional autopilot right here. Inside, I'm a mess, making running down inner me's face, as I hide in a corner, doubled over in pain. But outside? I'm angry, but professional. I'll do my job until the end.

"I didn't...what are the keys?"

"As I said, go do you, Ryder. They're to a place I have for clients in Murray Hill. It's Tudor City Place between East Forty First and Second. Nothing much but rich people and the UN, but it's private and not happening in the way you like."

He glances at the keys and then at me. "Punishment?"

"No. It's for clients to use on the downlow if they need to. Use it. Just...just don't report in. I don't need to hear about who you're banging."

Ryder nods tightly. "You want me to fuck other people?"

"Have orgies for all I care. Keep out of the papers for the next month and you'll sail home free. That advice is for free. So use it. Fuck all the women you want."

"Fine," he says lowly. "I will."

The words are a knife edge slicing through bone. "And we're not friends. I can't be friends with you, Ryder."

"So if I do the noble thing and walk so I don't screw things up—"

"Noble?" I hiss the word. "There's nothing noble about this. About what you did, about what you said. It's half assed, and it's all for your precious cock. You want your cake and you want to eat it as well. But you can't. And I'm not a cake."

"I have no idea what you're talking about."

"Of course you don't, Ryder. That's the problem. You didn't try. You give me a wonderful night and then decide you can't change, so you go and deliberately flirt with someone you don't want to send me a message—one I got, by the way—and then you come after me and offer me nothing but more half-assed words."

Something wet is on my face and with rising horror, I swipe the tear away.

"Don't—"

"It's frustration, nothing more. Am I hurt? Yes. Of course I am. I'm not you. I don't use my body as a trinket the way you do. I wanted you, I had...feelings...and you just trampled them down because you don't know if you can keep your dick in your pants."

Oh, God. I'm a fucking idiot.

I know what's wrong with me.

I've gone and done the thing I didn't think I would do with him. This isn't a crush. This is unforgivable.

This is love.

And he's not willing to be capable in the right way back.

"I think," I say quietly, "you should go now. You're never going to change, Ryder. We both know this."

He's pale. Very pale and he stares hard at me.

I want him to step up. I want him to say he's willing to try.

"We'll still see this through, the job?"

"Yes, Ryder. We will. I'm a professional."

"Good."

"Great."

Silence stretches thin and cold.

"That it, Elliot?"

"Yes. You're not about to change, Ryder. Are you?"

I want him to say yes. I want him to give me the keys back and offer me the world.

Actually, no. I don't want the world. Just him.

I want him to say he's not going, that this isn't the end.

I want him to say he loves me.

But he doesn't.

Ryder steps back. "No. I don't change, Elliot. Not in the long term. And you don't need to see it through to the end." He tosses the keys and catches them. "I think I got this."

"You'll let me just go?"

"Yes." He half takes another step, but stops. "And you? You'll let me take the keys and walk out the door."

"I gave them to you."

"Fine. Goodbye, Elliot."

Ryder turns and walks out the door, shattering my heart in to a million, bleeding pieces.

Chapter Twenty-Nine

RYDER

"Go away, King, I'm not in the mood."

My brother looks me up and down, frowning. It's been a day since I parted ways with Elliot and when I say I'm not in the mood, I mean it.

"Well aren't you the bundle of joy. How did the last board meeting go?"

King pushes past me and into my loft, looking about.

I sigh. "Fine. Jenson told me privately it's in the bag."

"Jenson said that?" He raises a brow.

"He didn't use those words. But the family company is saved, so you lot can work out who won the bet. I lost the girl, and you'll be getting your letter on your birthday."

"That's a few months away. I'm thinking of hiring someone to look into it, the jewels, I mean, find out what they can. Because I'm not really willing to jump through hoops." He moves into the living room and helps himself to a drink from the bar. "It's after five and it's been a long fucking day."

"It's been a long fucking four weeks," I mutter, rubbing my chest where this thing inside burns from the whole blow out with Elliot.

My brother leans against the bar. "You look like shit. What's this about the girl?"

"Nothing. You lot can work that bet out amongst yourselves, too."

My phone starts to ring and I pull it out and frown, but ignore the call. What I need is to get the fuck away from prying family. What I need is to make myself feel better. And the call...

"What happened, Ry? I've never seen you worked up over a woman before. Well, maybe that time on school vacation."

"I was twelve."

He smiles. "So?"

"I'm a fuck up, okay? And Elliot knows who and what I am and that means it would never work."

Suddenly, King holds up a hand and sets down his glass. "Woah, back up there. You like to screw around, but you don't hurt people. And what do you mean it would never work? Did Manhattan's last great lover fall?"

"No."

"That was a little quick, Ry." Kingston comes up to me and gives my arm a hard squeeze. And by hard, it hurts. "You need to wake up, Ryder. And fast. If you have feelings for her, don't hide behind what you do, or have done. Unless you're still fucking about."

"I haven't since...since before all this started."

"But," he says, "you fucked her."

"If this is your way of winning the secondary bet, asswipe, you—"

"I really don't give a shit about what amounts to a few pennies. I actually care about you. Strange, I know. But you're my little brother, and I'm stuck with you. Listen, if you like her, go see what happens. You never know until you try."

My chest tightens and my throat is clogged. "Would you?"

"I've had actual relationships, Ry. I'm not in the market for one, but I've had them. And this isn't about me. It's about you."

Yeah, it's about me being a fucking fool over a damn woman. I swear that's pity in his eyes.

"It's done. And I'm good."

"If you say so." He checks his watch. "I have an appointment. But think about what I said." King strides to the door and then stops. "Oh, be ready for the others. They're really into this bet."

That's why I end up in Murray Hill. I really don't need a repeat whatever the fuck that was from Hud and Mag. So I get the fuck out of dodge.

The place is nice, I guess. Bland. Tasteful. Something that will suit anyone because it doesn't offend. And I almost go to text something about it to Elliot when I remember.

Remember she's done with me.

Couldn't even give me a chance to explain. Couldn't even take into account I don't know what the hell I'm doing. Couldn't forgive me for a mistake, something she saw clean through.

I suck in a breath and poke about and make a drink. I'm in the mood for tequila but there's whiskey so I pour that straight up and swallow it down, relishing its sweet burn.

Elliot saw clean through it and came up with the wrong conclusion. And I...I didn't push to get it right.

What was the point?

I am a fuck up. I'm going to fuck up.

My phone starts again and this time I send a text with this address.

Lacey Fox is hot as all get out and she's been calling and texting me for days.

When she arrives, there are tear marks on her face, but even so, she's perfect. Right down to the tight clothes that show me everything I've been missing. All that sweet, ripe flesh.

I don't want it.

"Why did you change your mind, Ryder?" she asks.

I shrug. "You sounded upset in your message and there are only so many apologies I can take."

I'm playing with fire. I know that. But as she accepts the drink I give her, the story unspools. How she was coerced into the story.

"Shit, Lacey. You caused me a world of problems."

She looks down, and then up at me. "I didn't lie about the marriage. We're not together. It's a publicity thing and when you looked at me I was gone. No one's looked at me like that in a long time. Like they see me."

All the things Elliot said about me come back. "I didn't. Not in the way you want. But I saw someone I liked the look of. It's water under the bridge."

"I can release a statement about—"

"Lacey, whatever you do, promise you'll leave my name out of it."

I'm not naïve. I know this could backfire. But this is in private.

"I'm just alone, you know."

"Yeah."

I'm not going to bond with her, that's not smart and, well...neither is she. But she's nice and she's gorgeous and she can make a man forget his troubles.

"Can I use the bathroom?"

I point her in the direction, it's hard to miss as the place is small.

Slowly, I sit on the sofa and lean back closing my eyes. What the fuck am I doing? I don't really want to talk to her and I don't know if anything can make me forget my trouble. This place doesn't have enough whiskey for that.

Thing is, I wanted Elliot to tell me not to leave, to tell me she believed in me. Even if I hadn't done anything to make her say that, wasn't that something relationships had? Belief?

I go completely still. I want her to believe in me and want me enough.

Me. I've never in my life been unsure like I have been through all this. And it's Elliot. It's all her fault. She makes the ground shift beneath my feet. She unnerves and excites me and makes everything different.

And...she doesn't think I'm good enough for her.

She's right.

But if I'm being shut out of her life, punished, I might well do the crime. After all, Elliot believes all I want is to fuck women and there's one here. One who'd be more than happy to fuck me again.

I open my eyes and pull my phone out of my pocket, unlocking it. There's a text I set up to go out if I needed the SOS right at the beginning of all this and—

"Ryder."

"Yeah?" I look up, and I press the key on the screen without thinking.

Oh. Holy fucking shit.

Lacey Fox is naked. And she's waxed and buffed and spent even more money to make her perfection shine.

She sashays over to me and climbs on my lap and this is why Elliot doesn't want me.

It comes with horrible clarity as I put my hands on her hips, dropping my phone.

Why the fuck would a woman like Elliot believe in me, want me when women do this? Some women, I amend. The kind of woman I usually screw about with. The ones who want sex and aren't overly fussed with more, or if they are, don't say it.

"Uh, Lacey?"

"Yes...?" She slides her fingers through my hair and rubs those gravity defying breasts against me.

"What are you doing?"

"That should be obvious."

She goes in to kiss me and I lift her from me and put her down. I'm not even turned on. There's a throw on the back of the sofa and I grab it, shaking it out and tucking it about her neck.

I feel like a complete idiot.

She's hot, if given a helping hand from modern plastic surgery and fillers and all the rest of the shit out there. There's no denying she's fucking hot. And she's willing. This is also a private location, designed for this kind of thing so no one else will know and...I'm not turned on.

All I can think about is Elliot.

I appreciate the female form that's very naked next to me, but I don't want that female. At all.

I blow out a long breath. "I think you got the wrong idea."

"No, Ryder Sinclair asked me over. I know what that means."

I rub my eyes. "You kept calling. And texting. You wanted to talk. You sounded upset. I thought... I thought maybe you needed a space to breathe, and I thought if you wanted to talk to me you could."

"I'm here and I'm not in the mood to talk," she says her words practically a purr.

"Thing is, I'm not in the mood for getting down and dirty. There's someone else."

The moment those words appear, I know it's true and what they mean. It's not just I like Elliot. I have actual deep feelings for her. And I've been an ass.

A scared little boy hiding behind his reputation.

Lacey walks her fingers up my arm. "We forgive each other, right? I used you to push the fame of me and my fake husband. And it worked. I feel bad, and you used me for sex."

"I'm pretty sure we used each other for sex and I didn't sign up to be fodder."

"You have me now. I'm very adventurous, you know that."

"Yeah, but the thing is, I don't want you. I want her."

"So? Pretend I'm her. I really don't care. I just want to feel and feel wanted."

She leans over and tries to kiss me again and I'm pushing her away when someone clears their throat.

Elliot.

I know that disapproving sound anywhere.

"I think," Elliot says, "you should go."

"Her?" Lacey frowns. "It's her, isn't it? You love her."

"I don't do love."

The words come, empty, automatic, and Elliot says, "He doesn't. I work for him."

Lacey gets up and goes back to the bathroom and gets dressed. She's about to leave when Elliot stops her. "One word of you being here and I'll destroy your career. Any career. You'll be flipping burgers and poor when I'm done with you. So this is between the three of us." She pulls a card from her bag. "My lawyer. There'll be an NDA waiting for you by nine a.m. tomorrow. If you don't call tonight, and don't turn up and sign tomorrow, I'll start thinking you like smelling like fast food grease, the kind in the middle of nowhere pit stop grease."

Lacey runs like she just spoke to an evil demon and I'm thinking she might be right.

I don't think I've been impressed by anyone like I am now.

"How long were you there?"

"Long enough," Elliot says.

I start to smile.

"Don't you fucking dare."

The hope that started dies and I get it. We're really done. No trial. Just the sentence. And it's what I deserve for being a grade A asshole.

"You text me to come and save you?" She's jabbing her finger at me. "Why would you do that?"

"You tell me."

"No," she says, suddenly quietly, "you tell me. You had a reason."

"Because I can't change and I need you to keep me out of trouble?" She doesn't answer. "You know that."

"No, Ryder, I don't. I was in the neighborhood, so I was there a long time."

"And you thought I'd do it, didn't you?" I'm furious at the world, at myself, at her for being right. "You think I can't change and that's why you don't want me."

"You're being a child."

"I know." And I am and everything is hurting inside me. I'm so fucking screwed up over Elliot.

Every time I open my mouth the wrong things come out. The more I try and fix things the worse I make them. And I had a naked woman trying to hump me and she's not mad.

"Why aren't you angry?"

"I'm fucking furious, Ryder. Do not mistake how I am right now. I'm ready to burn things down."

"Because you think I can't change."

"No. Because you're an idiot. Worse, you're a self-destructive coward who hides behind his stupid reputation instead of trusting himself and me. You're a moron for inviting her over. What did you think she'd do? Have tea?"

"And if I can't change?"

"You can, if you want, Ryder. It's up to you."

"And you, Elliot? Do I get you?"

She walks up to me. "You don't deserve me, Ryder. I've helped you, given you all the tools you need. Or I should say, helped you find them and what do you do? Sabotage. You can be the man you are inside, but that depends on which one you think you are. The biggest man whore on the planet who's charming and funny, and ruthless and smart; or a man who is all those things without the need to nail anything that moves. It's up to you. But you need to do that. Not me. I'm not your crutch. I don't want to be."

I cross my arms. "So you'd be fine if I had a plethora of hot chicks panting for me?"

"Do what you want." She stops, blinking hard. "Would it matter if I wasn't okay with that?"

I don't answer because she's just unpacked a world at my feet.

"It's your life, your hands, Ryder. Goodbye."

Elliot turns and leaves and I don't go after her.

I've just been hit hard by what she's been saying. More by what I am. Beyond a coward who wanted her to hold my hand and make things easy.

That's not her job. I get that now.

It's my job to fight. And hard.

Because what just hit me is this: I didn't need her to save me from Lacey. I didn't want Lacey. I just wanted to see if Elliot would come. And she did. Because that's her. Elliot is more than I'm worth. She's way better than me. She shines.

And she's the one.

She's why I'm not interested in fucking anyone else.

She's why I realize I'll never be interested in fucking anyone else.

Every time I see another woman, it's Elliot I compare her to. Elliot I think about.

Fuck me.

I'm in love with her.

And I fucked it up by not even trying to fight. I've had it easy for so long, I fought myself rather than fight for her.

I wouldn't want me, either.

But I'm a selfish son of a good and devious woman.

I need to see Elliot. Now.

Heading out the door, I call, but it's straight to voicemail.

In my taxi to her offices, I still have voicemail. So I call the damn office.

Lena answers.

"I need you to put me through to Elliot. It's Ryder."

"Oh," she says. "She's gone. Left town."

I royally fucked up.

Chapter Thirty

ELLIOT

My knees go weak as he steps out of the car.

Why I'm here at Ryder's place is beyond stupid and into the realm of masochism. I'm meant to be gone. I took the day off and had some last minute things to do in Murray Hill, which is why I got to observe that lovely scene of the spectacular and naked starlet climb all over him.

And his well-handled rejection of said naked woman.

And yet, Ryder still managed to fuck it up with me.

He wants a crutch, not someone where there might be a future.

So...masochism has me here.

But I can't leave without seeing him.

His walk slows to a stop as he sees me. "Elliot?"

"That's my name."

Ryder climbs the steps to his door and lets us in. "I thought...I thought I'd fucked up."

"You did." I stop in the entrance way as he shuts the door behind me. "I'm leaving. I've a vacation planned and I moved it up. I can't be here anymore. Not for a while. Any loose ends, Andre will handle them."

"I'm paying you."

"You have paid me," I corrected. "And I'm delegating. I know you're getting your necklace, which will look very pretty on you. And you saved the company. So, Andre can handle the loose ends, if there are any."

He nods, and he rubs the back of his neck. "It would look better on you, Elliot."

My body starts to tingle. Not for some jewel, but what he's saying behind it. "It's not mine."

"I fucked up, big time. I didn't fight for you. I wasn't honest. This is all new for me. You are like nothing I've ever known in my life. You're my friend, and someone I want to spend weeks on end in bed with. You make me so angry and happy and unsure of myself. You make me secure and you make me feel like I have no idea what I'm doing and I don't get how that happens. Except, maybe it's to do with how you just make me feel, Elliot."

I keep the hope that's trying to get free from escaping, because these aren't the words I want to hear. Not completely. "Why did you ask her to Murray Hill?"

"I don't know."

"Sure you do."

"She sounded sad? She kept calling? I wanted...maybe I wanted to see what would happen. Maybe I was so fucking angry you rejected me I thought I'd do it."

The words slap me, hard. "I see."

"I thought maybe I could, but that wasn't why. I don't know why. Shit, I wasn't even interested in her at all. Elliot, I think you broke me."

I start laughing even as tears burn my eyes and I'm not sure if they're happy or sad. "I didn't break you."

Ryder wipes a finger under my eye. "Don't cry, Elliot. I'm not worth it."

"You are to me. That's the problem. Maybe I came here because I wanted to see...to see you, to see why you called."

"Maybe deep down it was a test," he says, sounding a little dazed.

"Maybe."

"To see if I could change, not for you to save me." Ryder takes my face in his hands. "I actually was so fucking gobsmacked when she walked out naked—I'd been sitting there thinking about you, obsessing might be the word, and I had that text out…I wrote it as an SOS right back at the beginning. And maybe I wanted to see if you'd turn up—I just hit send."

"And I show up."

"You're not a crutch, not like that. I want you to be a lot of things with me. All of them. And I want to be all those with you."

Now I reach up, and run my fingers over those soft lips of his, the ones I dream about. "For what it's worth, I don't think you can change, I think you have."

"Because of you."

"Maybe," I say. "And maybe because of you, too. I see you, Ryder. All of you. You're more than this ridiculously beautiful face of yours. You're more than being amazing in bed. You're more than charm and magnetism. You can be awkward. I know I am, and I like that you can be, too. It's charming if we're not arguing over you putting your foot in it. Your fucking up like that is what people do. It might cause you grief, make you feel like you're in Dante's hell—"

"Seventh circle, usually."

I start to smile because I can't contain the hope, it's blooming like it's got a life of its own. "It makes you human, Ryder."

"So what's your excuse for your perfection?"

"I'm not perfect."

"To me, how you are is. You might frustrate the fuck out of me, but I don't want you to be anything other than you are, Elliot."

"That's good, because I can't be. I'm not great with the limelight. I hate half the events we went to. Except…except they weren't so bad with you. And I like being in your light."

"It's the other way around. I'm better in yours."

I go up on my toes and kiss him softly. "Ryder, I'm trying to say I'm not expecting anything from you. But I want you to know I appreciate you." The words of love are there, but I'm not letting them out. And whatever happens, I need to tell him this. Then I can go. No matter what this hope inside thinks. "I get some people just see the surface. Gorgeous rich man and nothing else. Not me."

"You see the monster?"

"You're an idiot. No, I see you. You like beautiful things, but you understand them. You saw what my plants are with me, and with my art deco furniture, you know what it is, the beauty side of old things that are loved. You appreciate not the monetary value but the aesthetics and that's rare."

"I appreciate you, Elliot. More than you know," he says quietly.

"I'm not beautiful or anything—"

"You are," he says, releasing me and taking my hand, bringing it to his lips and pressing a kiss against my palm. "You're beautiful and sexy and you're the hottest thing I've met. I can talk with you. I can tell you anything. I can just relax with you."

And yet, he doesn't tell me what I long to hear and maybe he doesn't feel how I do. Maybe he—

"I love you, Elliot."

He's shaking and I start, too.

"I've never said that to anyone before, outside family. I've never loved before and I think I might have for a long time, I just went about it wrong. I mean, it takes a bit to work out what the complicated thing you're feeling is. At least for me. And you don't need to love me back. You can walk out the door, because I sure as fuck don't deserve you. Will I try and stop you? Yes. Will I try and wear you down and win you and spend a life taking whatever I can get with you? Absolutely."

Ryder meets my gaze. "Basically, I'm trying to say I'm head over heels in love with you, and I don't want anyone but you. I love you."

"Really?" The hope is back swooping, flying singing and my heart is so full and big and I can't stop the sudden wild happiness from spilling inside.

"Yes."

I start to cry. Not sobs, but tears definitely fall and I can't help it. I know what those other tears were now. Pure hope and that's morphed right into happy. "You love me?"

"With everything I am."

"I love you, too. I am so in love with you I make myself sick."

"I know you don't trust me, but—"

"I trust you, Ryder."

"Even when I don't trust myself?"

"Don't push it," I say, looping my arms around his neck. "That's fear. You're your number one fan, you do trust yourself. You just were finding your feet and you never did anything. You had a naked woman begging to sleep with you."

"She wasn't you." He kisses me soft and slow and sweet and then looks at me, a wicked light in his eyes. "Or maybe I'm lying."

"No. I know your tells."

"Really?"

"I'll never tell."

I kiss him again and he holds me tight, kissing me back like I'm the most precious thing in his life. "You know, you're worth more than the company and the necklace. Without you, it's empty."

A Spice Girls song starts and he reluctantly pulls free. "My mother."

He waits for the phone to stop ringing. Then when it beeps, he listens to the voicemail. Ryder hangs up and shoves his phone away. "Holy fucking hell, Elliot. That was her congratulating me and her saying if I don't seal the deal with the best thing that's happened to me—you—I'm in trouble, but Kingston's piece is missing. She has the necklace but the last piece and his quest are gone; not that I trust her or Jenson in this. My brother is not going to be happy. But this is in King's hands now. Oh no."

"What?" The look of annoyance on his face twists in me.

"I'm going to have to introduce you to my family."

"You don't have to."

"Well, it's going to be strange if they never meet my wife."

For a moment I can't speak. "Wife?"

"Yes. Maybe not tomorrow or next week, but I love you and I'm not letting you go, Elliot. Marry me. I want a life with my hot best friend. I want one that means something. With you."

"I never saw myself as getting married," I say, "but for you, I'll make an exception. And I don't think I want to let you go. After all, who knows what situations you'll get yourself into."

"I love you, Elliot. I'm going to spend my life showing you."

We kiss, and all that angst and twisting ourselves in knots seems miles away. If we could get through that, then we can get through anything. And now we know we love each other. And there's trust, it's going to be good. With Ryder by my side, we can do anything.

It's not just love. Because he's my best friend, too. And this feels right. It feels good.

It's forever.

It's that kind of deal, and he isn't the only one who changed, I did, too.

We changed for each other.

Because we found love.

This is the end of Ryder and Elliot's love story.
But the two, as well as all the other Sinclair brothers, return.
The series continues with the story of Kingston and Sadie and the grand finale of the Sinclairs and their legacy. The title is "Merciless Heir".
You can find the series here:
US: https://www.amazon.com/dp/B0D928VLH1
UK: https://www.amazon.co.uk/dp/B0D928VLH1

***

Or would you like to read my free enemies-to-lovers-romance "Date with Hate"?
Then, click here and subscribe and get your free copy instantly into your inbox:

https://sendfox.com/rebeccabaker

Afterword

Dear reader,

I really hope you enjoyed this story. If so, I would appreciate a short review on Amazon.

As an indie author, I don't have the resources of a major publisher, so this is the way you would support me the most.

***

You will look for contraceptives in vain in this book. Why is that? The story takes place in your imagination and should give you a carefree time and carefree reading pleasure.

In this world, all billionaires have six-packs and are really good in bed. STDs don't exist in this world.

My free romance novel

Would you like to read my free enemies-to-lovers-romance "Date with Hate"?

Then, click here and subscribe and get your free copy instantly into your inbox:

https://sendfox.com/rebeccabaker

Printed in Great Britain
by Amazon